The Sociology of Elites

CW01064647

The Sociology of Elites deals with the highly topical issue of the role of elites in society. In view of the continuing growth of the divide between the rich and the poor, people in many industrialized countries are asking questions about the responsibility of the elites for society. Are the activities of elites determined primarily by their responsibility for the common good of the population or by their interest in enlarging their own power and wealth?

In answering this question the book presents an overview of the most important sociological elite theories, ranging from the classics in the field – Mosca, Michels, and Pareto – to authors such as Lasswell, Dahrendorf, and Keller, and including the determinative critical elite theorists Bourdieu and Mills. The book also looks at the world's five largest industrialized nations the United States, France, Germany, the UK, and Japan – and shows through empirical analyses how the elites in the various countries, especially the political and economic elites, are recruited and how they cooperate with one another. Particular emphasis is put on the role played by educational institutions and the question of whether it is appropriate to speak of separate sectoral elites or of a ruling class.

Michael Hartmann is Professor of Sociology at the Technical University of Darmstadt, Germany.

Routledge studies in social and political thought

The Sociology of Elites

Michael Hartmann

Routledge
Taylor & Francis Group

LONDON AND NEW YORK

This translated edition first published 2007
by Routledge
2 Park Square, Milton Park, Abingdon, Oxon OX14 4RN

Simultaneously published in the USA and Canada
by Routledge
711 Third Avenue, New York, NY 10017

First issued in paperback 2012
Routledge is an imprint of the Taylor & Francis Group, an informa business

© 2004 Campus. Originally published as Elitesoziologie. Eine
Einführung by Campus Verlag GmbH. © Campus, Frankfurt a.M.
2004. All rights reserved.

Typeset in Garamond by Wearset Ltd, Boldon, Tyne and Wear

British Library Cataloguing in Publication Data
A catalogue record for this book is available from the British Library

Library of Congress Cataloging in Publication Data
A catalog record for this book has been requested

ISBN13: 978-0-415-65185-1 (pbk)
ISBN13: 978-0-415-41197-4 (hbk)
ISBN13: 978-0-203-96624-2 (ebk)

Contents

1 Introduction

The debate recently sparked by the German SPD on so-called elite universities has lent new impetus to the discussion on elites in Germany. All of a sudden politicians, managers, and journalists are demanding elite universities for Germany as well, calling, just about in unison, for a German Harvard or a German Princeton. The renowned American private elite universities have become the unquestioned model for aspirations to restructure Germany's university landscape, which in fact have already reached the planning stage. This partiality for the idea of the elite is not entirely new. Since the early 1990s it has attracted an ever-increasing measure of support from the leading German media as well as from prominent politicians and representatives of the business world. In their opinion Germany is in urgent need of capable and active elites if it is to keep pace with international competition and not decline into mediocrity.

The sustained barrages laid down by the media are starting to bear fruit among the population at large. While the majority are still critical or dismissive of the notion of elites, there is a constantly growing minority who embrace the idea. The *Frankfurter Allgemeine Zeitung* (FAZ), for instance, proudly reported last October that 54 percent of the German public were now in favor of promoting particularly gifted children in elite classes or elite schools, and that only 33 percent were still opposed to the idea. This is a remarkable change over a period of only a few years. Still, the majority of the population continues to feel ill at ease in view of the ongoing discussion over elites. The latter are still associated above all with unjustified privileges (such as the horrendous salaries, severance payments, and pension commitments awarded in the top echelons of Germany's large corporations) as well as with what continues to be perceived as the pretentiousness and arrogance of power. What people have in mind here are the more or less egregious escapades of people like the former CEO of Mannesmann, Klaus Esser, and the managing director of the Federal Employment Agency, Florian Gerster. To most people the conduct of top executives of this variety appears to be typical of elites. To cite a concrete example: When, during court proceedings in Düsseldorf devoted to seemingly exaggerated severance payments awarded to the members of Mannesmann's executive and supervisory boards, the Deutsche Bank's board spokesman, Joseph Ackermann, stated, with a smirk on his face, that Germany was, "the only country in which people who create values are taken to court," he was confirming this impression, albeit unwittingly.

When the subject of elites comes up, the proponents are always in a hurry to affirm that under no circumstances are they speaking of "natural" elites, that is, of elites that are merely seeking to defend their privileges. On the contrary, the argument generally goes, the aim is to create meritocratic elites or, as they are sometimes called, value elites. But what is behind all these terms? What is meant by the term elites? Do they really exist, and if so, who belongs to them? Sociology has been attempting to find an answer to all these questions for over a century now. The history of sociology's concern with the subject has a changeful and varied history of its own. There have been peaks, for example at the turn of the nineteenth to the twentieth century, in the 1930s, after the Second World War, or in recent years, but there have also been protracted phases of widespread disinterest. But the issue has never completely disappeared from the agenda of sociological inquiry. Who the leaders of a society are, how they lead, and where they come from – these are questions that have – more or less – always fired the imagination of sociological observers.

If, with a view to obtaining an initial overview and clarification of the concept, we start out by consulting a standard German encyclopedia such as Brockhaus or Meyer, we find the following definition. The term "elite" has its roots in the French word *élire* (select), has been in common usage in France since the seventeenth century, and was adopted into the German language in the eighteenth century. There "elite" is defined as a social group distinguished by "its high levels of qualification and its ability and willingness to achieve" (*Brockhaus Encyclopedia*) or by its "particular value or performance" (*Meyer's Encyclopedic Lexicon*); elites are furthermore seen as groups that have a decisive influence on the development of society.

Viewed historically, the concept of the elite was developed in the eighteenth century by the aspiring French bourgeoisie as a democratic rallying cry in the struggle to break the hegemony of aristocracy and clergy. Individual achievement as opposed to family origins was to be the decisive requirement for assuming leading positions in society. The nineteenth century experienced profound changes in the use of the term elite, with the concept now serving as a contrast to the term mass. The middle classes, and with them the middle-class academic intelligentsia of the time, were deeply troubled about the phenomenon of the urban masses which had evolved as a result of the population explosion in Europe and went hand in hand with the development of the industrial working class. In their eyes, the political unrest and revolutionary aspirations of the masses served only to endanger the ruling order. The classic elite theories formulated against this background by Mosca, Michels, and Pareto,[1] with their contrast between the elite and the masses, were later to provide an important ideological basis for the rise of fascism in Italy and Germany. The conviction of these theorists that a small elite was bound to dominate the large majority was later used by the fascist parties as a central justification of the principle of authoritarian leadership.

The concept of elite was discredited by fascism and the conflict with the socialist camp, and it was comprehensively redefined after the Second World War. After an initial revival (above all in Germany) of the concept of the value elite, with the term elite now understood (at least in public pronouncements) as a minority distinguished by certain moral and ethical qualities, it was not long before the German social sciences, and later the general public, began to adopt the functionalist definition of elites current in the US. This view is still the predominant one today, although recently the classic dichotomy of elite and mass has gained growing currency there.[2]

According to this functionalist theory there is no longer one single elite, the minority of the chosen few on the one side with the mass on the other; nor is there a ruling class. There are only functional or sectoral or subelites whose members are distinguished from the rest of the population by the top positions they hold in various sectors of society, and which give them a decisive influence on the development of society. The insinuation is that members of elites have attained their positions solely on the grounds of their individual performance.[3] What we have here is, then, performance-based positional or functional elites (the terms used here vary somewhat).

For functionalist elite research these include the holders of the highest positions in politics (in Germany these would be members of the federal and state governments, the executive committees of the political parties and parliamentary factions), administration (state secretaries, heads of ministerial departments, presidents of important authorities), business (boards of directors and in some cases members of the supervisory boards of large corporations, presidents and vice-presidents of major associations), the judiciary (federal judges), the media (owners, publishers, managing directors, directors, managers, and editors-in-chief of the important media), the academy (university presidents and directors of major research institutes), the military (generals and admirals), and labor unions (chairmen and their deputies). In essence, all researchers concerned with elites, including critical researchers, agree on the makeup of this list. The only controversial point is the inclusion of the top-level labor union posts. While it is true that they are included in all major German studies on elites, labor-union leaders are seen as part of the social elite neither by critical theorists such as Mills and Bourdieu nor by functionalist-oriented researchers like Suzanne Keller.

Keller may serve as an example of the fact that it is not only theorists like Bourdieu – with their view of elites as closely intertwined with the concept of the ruling class – who oppose the classification of leading labor unionists as belonging to elites. In view of the actual power relations in society, other, less critical authors are also ill at ease with this classification. This is easy to understand considering the influence of the labor-union leadership on the making of political decisions these days. The recent search of the German metal workers' union (IG Metall) for a new president illustrates the true position of top-ranking labor unionists. All union personnel managers who were asked to apply for the post declined the offer. In labor-union circles it was said that they all gave as a reason the fact that a move of this kind would involve not only a (more or less) tangible drop in income but would also mean a loss of social prestige.

A second proviso is also necessary here. If we take a closer look at the matter, we see that the media elite cannot be characterized as a separate elite in its own right. Since the breakthrough of commercial providers in countries which two or three decades ago had only publicly owned broadcasting corporations, the media landscape has come to be dominated in all leading industrialized nations by large private corporations (such as Bertelsmann, Disney, or Time-Warner) or by media tycoons (like Berlusconi or Murdoch). As the remaining public-sector media institutions are increasingly dominated by political interests, it is not really possible to speak any longer of the media elite playing a really independent role. If we furthermore consider, first, the marked loss of influence the military elite has experienced since the Second World War (the objections of the US and British general staffs to a war on Iraq had no noteworthy influence either in the phase leading up to the war or on the course of the war itself), and, second, the clearly visible dependence of today's academic elite on industry and politics, we cannot fail to note that, in the end, the top representatives of business, politics, administration, and the judiciary constitute the most important social elites today. It is for this reason that the major focus of the empirical part of the present study will be on these groups.

The present introduction to the sociology of elites consists of two major sections. Chapters 2 to 4 provide an outline and critical review of the sociological discussion on elites. To this end we will take a closer look at both the classic theories of Michels, Mosca, and Pareto as well as at the most important functionalist approaches (from Lasswell and Kaplan and Kornhauser via Dahrendorf, Stammer, and Keller to Hoffmann-Lange and Field and Higley) and the most important critical theories of elites (Mills and Bourdieu). Chapters 5 and 6 are then devoted to, first, an empirical analysis of the mechanisms used to recruit candidates for the most influential elite positions (in particular the role played by educational institutions in this process) and, second, the relations of the important elites both among one another and with the rest of society, as exemplified by the world's five largest industrialized nations (Germany, France, Great Britain, Japan, and the US). Finally, we will, in this context, take a close look at the above-mentioned differences and deficits inherent in research on elites today with an eye to formulating some possible approaches that bring more clarity to several central points at issue.

2 Elite and mass

In its formative years the discussion on elites in the social sciences was inseparable from the discussion on what was then known as the masses. In this debate elite and mass represented two sides of the same coin: elite was the positive concept, mass the negative. The classic studies on the concept of the elite, by Mosca (1896), Pareto (1916), and Michels (1911), were published almost at the same time as Le Bon's classic, *The Crowd: A Study of the Popular Mind* (1895).

It is no coincidence that all the fundamental books on this complex issue appeared within about 20 years of one another, around the turn of the nineteenth to the twentieth century. At that time the middle classes, and with them the middle-class academic intelligentsia, were deeply concerned about the phenomenon of the urban masses which had emerged throughout Europe in the course of the nineteenth century as a result of the population explosion there. Distinctly reduced mortality rates, increases in birth rates, and gradual improvements in living standards achieved in connection with industrialization had led to hitherto unparalleled growth in the population of Europe. Whereas Europe's population had grown only very slowly, from roughly 80 million to approximately 110 million, between 1300 and 1700, it grew far more rapidly, by almost 80 million to roughly 188 million, in the eighteenth century, in order then to reach wholly new dimensions in the nineteenth century. Around 1850 there were about 267 million people living in Europe, but by 1900 this figure already exceeded 400 million. Annual population growth amounted to about 10 percent and was thus more than three times as high as it was in the period from 1650 to 1750 (Bergeron *et al.* 1969 [1998]: 230–5; Dülmen 1982 [1998]: 20–1; Palmade 1975 [1998]: 10–15; Romano and Tenenti 1967 [1998]: 14–15).

At the same time, Europe also found itself faced with unprecedented urbanization. This development, however, began (with the exception of Great Britain) only about half a century later. The number of cities with a population of over 100,000 had more than doubled from 22 to 47 in the period between 1800 and 1850, and the percentage of the overall population living in urban centers had also grown from roughly 3 percent to about 5 percent, with England alone accounting for one-third of this increase

(Bergeron *et al.* 1969 [1998]: 232), and thus the actual dynamics of urbanization were not really felt in the rest of Europe until the second half of the nineteenth century. This was true in particular for Germany, where the growth of urban centers reached an incredible pace. Within only four decades, between the foundation of Reich in 1871 and the year 1910, the number of big cities increased sixfold from eight to 48, while the population of these cities increased sevenfold. If in 1871 fewer than one in 20 Germans lived in a city, this figure had increased to more than one in five, or 21.3 percent, by 1910 (Wehler 1995: 512). The capital, Berlin, alone had a population of 2.07 million in 1914 as compared with only 826,000 40 years earlier. Even in France, where population growth was far lower than in any other major European country (only 40 percent between 1801 and 1884), the development was still impressive. If in 1846 there were only three towns other than Paris with a population of over 100,000, by 1886 the figure had risen to seven. In 1886 the population of Paris, the truly dominant European capital, was 2.345 million, compared with only 945,000 in mid-century (Armengaud 1986: 169–70). The growth of Europe's cities was paralleled by the emergence of densely populated regions such as the industrial areas of northern England or the Ruhr region in Germany.

This rapid urbanization was accompanied by the rise of the industrial working class. While this process was already well advanced in Britain by 1850 – every fourth employed person was a worker at this juncture – it did not get underway until the second half of the nineteenth century in other western and central European countries. Once again, this development proceeded at a strikingly rapid pace in Germany. The share of factory workers and miners in the overall labor force doubled from about 6 to 12 percent between 1850 and 1871, and by 1907 this group accounted for almost one-third of the overall labor force (Wehler 1995: 141–2, 773–5). These developments were at the same time accompanied by a concentration of workers in large factories. Within only 25 years, between 1882 and 1907, the percentage of workers employed in companies with a workforce of over 50 rose from 22.8 to 42.4 percent. To illustrate the extent of the changes which were shaking the basic structures of society at that time: In the mining sector more than 96 percent of workers were employed in operations of this size; in the industrial manufacturing sector the percentage of companies employing over 1,000 workers rose from 1.9 to 4.9 percent; and for mining the equivalent percentage rose from 33 to 58.2 (Hohorst *et al.* 1975: 75). The industrial proletariat had unmistakably entered the historical arena. Many contemporary observers saw in the rise of the masses a twofold threat to the existing social order. The existence of such masses, thus an opinion widespread among the middle classes, and here particularly among the intelligentsia, not only fostered growth in crime but also constituted a fundamental threat to the ruling order by fomenting political unrest and revolutionary aspirations. As far as the second point is concerned, the actions of the urban masses in the French Revolution of 1789 and the later revolutionary uprisings of 1848 (Germany, France, Italy, Austria-Hungary) up to 1905 (Russia) appeared to leave no doubt. When the masses were swept up in a political movement, their goal seemed inevitably to be the revolution of the existing capitalist system.

The stronger the influence of the working class became, the greater was the fear of revolution, particularly in view of the fact that the workers' parties and labor unions in continental Europe had unanimously stated their goal to be socialism and hence the overthrow of the bourgeois order. Accordingly, the term masses came to be understood to mean primarily the proletarian masses. The boundaries between mass and class became increasingly blurred in this process. Fear was particularly great in countries which, like France (1789, 1830, 1848, and in 1871 the Paris Commune), already had made considerable experience with revolutionary uprisings, or like Germany and Italy, which had completed processes of nation-building in parallel to the process of industrialization; here, as a result, attempts to establish a middle-class-dominated parliamentary system coincided with the development of a working class that was visibly growing in strength. At any rate, in the widespread opinion of the middle classes no good was to be expected of the masses.

2.1 *The Crowd: A Study of the Popular Mind* (Gustave Le Bon)

It was to this middle-class attitude that the sensational success of Gustave Le Bon's[1] 1895 book *Psychologie des foules* (English: *The Crowd: A Study of the Popular Mind*) was due.[2] Le Bon succeeded in relating his analysis to the fears of middle-class intellectual circles and fueling them with what appeared to be an exact scientific justification. This is made very clear in the introduction to the book, which Le Bon entitled "The Era of Crowds." This chapter heading is itself characteristic in that it appealed precisely to the sentiments of the great majority of readers, who saw in the massification of society the first signs of the decline of the West, or at least of Western culture.[3] Le Bon comes to the central points of his analysis in the first pages of the book. While, he notes, up to the end of the eighteenth century the "rivalries of sovereigns" were the driving force behind events, with the opinion of the masses playing as good as no role whatever, the tables had turned completely within the span of only one century. The "voice of the people" was now, he continued, the decisive factor, dictating how monarchs were to act. The mass, whose demands amounted to no less than the utter destruction "of society as it now exists" in favor of a "primitive communism," was all the more determined to act, the less it was capable of reason. The mission of the masses in history, Le Bon argues, had lain essentially in the destruction, not in the creation, of ancient civilizations. Until now civilizations had, he claims, only been created and led "by a small intellectual aristocracy." The rule of the masses, however, was, in Le Bon's view, tantamount to a phase of dissolution, because civilization required traits such as reason, impulse control, or, in general terms, an "elevated degree of culture," all of which the masses, "left to themselves, have invariably shown themselves incapable of realising." It was, he goes on, therefore to be feared that this process would repeat itself for the then dominant culture, "since want of foresight has in succession overthrown all the barriers that might have kept the crowd in check" (Le Bon 1895 [1896]: xv–xx).

Although in the further course of his analysis Le Bon does come to some differentiated, albeit frequently self-contradictory, assessments of mass behavior, it is his introductory remarks which set the tone for the overall work. The mass, distinguishable in essence from the sum of its individual members in that it forms "a single being" and is subject to the "*law of the mental unity of masses*" (ibid.: 2; emphasis in the original), is to Le Bon rough, barbaric, easily influenced, impulsive, excitable, lacking in reason, imperious, and only under very specific conditions "capable of morality" – and then, by reason of its unbridled impulses, only for a short period of time. Thus it "is fortunate for the progress of civilization that the power of crowds only began to exist when the great discoveries of science and industry had already been effected" (ibid.: 42), since their realization would have been impossible if democracy had already unfolded its full powers. As Le Bon writes in his chapter on the "Electoral Crowd," "civilisations" are only conceivable as "the work of a small minority of superior intelligences" (ibid.: 198).

In his comparison of "the small minority of superior intelligences" and the broad mass, Le Bon's observations resemble those made by Mosca, Pareto, and Michels on elite and mass. While it is true that in his book Le Bon uses neither the term elite nor the term ruling or political class, the reader is unlikely to overlook the substantive congruences between this and other passages. This is particularly evident where Le Bon analyzes the relationship between mass and leader. In his view the masses instinctively seek a leader. The mass, he claims, is "a servile flock that is incapable of ever doing without a master," one that always follows a strong-willed leader. The rule of leaders is accordingly "extremely despotic;" indeed it owes its authority "to this despotism alone" (ibid.: 118–21). Here, just as in his assessment of parliamentarism, Le Bon uses figures of argumentation which, at least in their core, but in some cases also in their concrete formulations (e.g. his statements on the role played by violence), bear resemblance to the three classic writers on the sociology of elites.

2.2 "The Ruling Class" (Gaetano Mosca)

Gaetano Mosca[4] was the first theorist to attempt an in-depth sociology of elites. His major work, *Elementi di Scienza Politica*, was published just one year after Le Bon's *Psychologie des foules* and was based chiefly on two works published in 1884 and 1887, *Sulla teoria dei Governi e sul Governo representa-*

tivo. Studi storici e sociali and *Le Constitutioni moderne*.[5] Mosca's key ideas find expression in the second chapter of his main work, entitled "The Ruling Class." This chapter begins with Mosca's most-quoted sentence:

> Among the constant facts and tendencies of the life of a state, one is so obvious that it is apparent to the most casual eye. In all societies – from societies that are very meagerly developed and have barely attained the dawnings of civilization, down to the most advanced and powerful societies – two classes of people appear – a class that rules and a class that is ruled. The first class, always the less numerous, performs all political functions, monoplizes power and enjoys the advantages that power brings, whereas the second, the more numerous class, is directed and controlled by the first, in a manner that is now more or less legal, now more or less arbitrary and violent, and supplies the first, in appearance at least, with material means of subsistence and with the instrumentalities that are essential to the vitality of the political organism.
>
> (Mosca 1896 [1939]: 50)

This universal principle is not, in Mosca's view, invalidated by universal suffrage and parliamentarism. In his chapter on suffrage he states explicitly that, despite appearances to the contrary, in a "representative system" there is, just as in any other form of government, "an organized minority" which "imposes its will on the diorganized majority" (ibid.: 154). Those elected are, he further notes, not as a rule the representatives of the majority, who simply delegate their power to them for a given period of time, but are part of the ruling minority. There is therefore no reason whatsoever to speak of government by the majority.[6]

Using the paired terms organized and unorganized, Mosca again refers to one of the two points which he made immediately after the basic proposition cited above and which he views as crucial evidence of the inevitability of the rule of the minority over the majority. This, as he noted there, is "inevitable" quite simply because, for one thing, the former are "organized" and the latter "unorganized." A minority, he continues, is, as it were, organized by definition, for the simple reason that it is easier for 100 people to "act in concert" than it is for 1,000. The larger the state, and hence the smaller the ruling minority in relation to the population, the easier it is as a consequence for the minority to secure its rule. The second reason Mosca cites is that ruling minorities generally consist of individuals, who are superior to the mass of the ruled in both material and intellectual terms (ibid.: 53). It is this superiority, together with moral prestige, which he sees as being the central means required to lead the masses (ibid.: 244).

At various points in the further course of his argument Mosca looks more closely into this issue. As far as the material aspect is concerned, his chief point is that whereas in earlier stages of development the key feature of the ruling class was its martial prowess, wealth has become its characteristic feature in advanced societies. For Mosca, wealth now constitutes the basis of political power. "[T]he people who rule are the rich rather than the brave," he succinctly remarks (ibid.: 58).[7] If wealth was originally founded on the possession of land, he claims, it is now being increasingly supplanted by money as a result of the development of trade and industry. Furthermore – and here Mosca is reverting to the thread of his argument on the importance of organization – mobile wealth in the form of money is generally superior to immobile wealth in the form of land, because the former is far easier to organize. It is, he goes on, relatively easy for large sums of money to become concentrated in the hands of individuals, with the result that a "few individuals" are in a position to control all of a country's major banks, transportation companies, or other major public corporations. The few who have hundreds of millions at their disposal "possess the most various resources for threatening or cajoling other interests however far-reaching, and for intimidating and corrupting . . . ministries, legislative bodies, newspapers" (ibid.: 147). Thus it is, he concludes, that "plutocracy" is the most powerful of all material forces.

As far as the "intellectual" superiority of the ruling minority is concerned, Mosca sees the major reason for it not in the biological inheritance of certain traits[8] but – and this is reminiscent of contemporary authors like Bourdieu – in their upbringing, in the passing down of behavior patterns and attitudes through the family, as well as in other background factors. He notes there are considerable inborn differences between individuals, "but more than anything else traditions and environmental influences are the things that keep them high, low or just average, in any large group of human beings" (ibid.: 64). This, he notes, is particularly true of positive character traits (such as courage in battle or endurance in defense), which are usually associated with the "higher classes."

His critique of biologistic patterns of interpretation leads Mosca to formulate a second basic proposition. Since the political class rules not by virtue of hereditary traits but on the basis of its possession of the "social forces" needed to attain the required intellectual and economic superiority and moral prestige, any change in these social forces (such as the rise of money as a new source of wealth) must also lead to changes in the composition of the political class. This, however, necessarily leads to conflicts over political power. It is hence, Mosca notes, possible to explain the whole of history of mankind as a "conflict between the tendency of dominant elements to monopolize political power and transmit possession of it by inheritance, and a tendency toward dislocation of old forces and an insurgence of new forces" (ibid.: 65).

In Mosca's view all political classes have an inherent desire to see their power placed on a de facto, or indeed on a legalized, footing of inheritability. Wealth and martial prowess, Mosca observes, are handed down through families in the form of traditions and direct inheritance; children are familiar with the practices of "high politics" from their early years on. Finally, as regards public offices, which are theoretically open to anyone passing an examination, the fact remains that the majority of the population lacks both the resources needed for the lengthy period of education and training required and the connections that would "set an individual promptly on the right road, enabling him to avoid the gropings and blunders that are inevitable when one enters an unfamiliar envionment without any guidance of support" (ibid.: 61).

At another point in his analysis Mosca states that relatively stable social structures inevitably favor efforts aimed at monopolization. Even in a parliamentary system the absence of major convulsions, be they of an internal or external nature, again and again paves the way for the offspring of the ruling class to "attain with increasing ease the posts that are now occupied by their fathers, and a little world apart would come into being, a clique of influential families into which it would be hard for newcomers to make their way" (ibid.: 260). This severely restricts the rise of able men from the lower classes. One crucial consequence of this development, Mosca notes, is a dangerous alteration in the composition of the ruling class, which would then "grow poorer and poorer in bold and aggressive characters and richer and richer in 'soft,' remissive individuals" (ibid.: 117).[9] While the lack of energy shown by individual members of the upper class in a developed society could, to a certain extent, be compensated for by their greater culture and wealth and their firm cohesion, in the long run, thus Mosca's analysis, the ruling class would no longer be in a position to respond adequately to impending threats. The political regime would collapse "at the first appreciable shock from the outside foe" (ibid.: 119).

The conflict between the ruling class's efforts at monopolization and the will of new forces to advance up the ladder can, in Mosca's view, be resolved at best temporarily in favor of the former. In the long run, he goes on, this is not possible, with the result that part of the lower classes will necessarily and permanently amalgamate with the upper classes. Indeed, should certain traits used by the political classes to rise to power lose significance, or vanish altogether, these classes (just as in the case of the Roman or Venetian aristocracy) would "inevitably" decline (ibid.: 65). In such a case the composition of the ruling class would inevitably change.

Further discussion of this problem constitutes an important, if not indeed the central, aspect of the six chapters which Mosca added to the first edition of his book in the second, revised edition of 1923. He starts out by noting generally that "the supreme heads of states have, in general, been able to leave enduring marks on history only when they have managed to take the initiative in timely reforms of ruling classes" (ibid.: 337). In the further course of his argument he defines more precisely than previously the efforts made to open or to close the ruling class as an aristocratic or, in the second case, democratic tendency (ibid.: 395). Both tendencies are always in play, he contends, although the democratic principle is normally effected through gradual "infiltration of elements from the lower into the higher classes," and rarely takes the shape of violent revolts (ibid.: 414). However, this process can only be considered a positive one – and Mosca goes as far as to formulate this as a rule – if those on the way up the social ladder are in possession of what is needed to "at once adopt the best qualities of the members." On the other hand, Mosca continues, the harmful case is given when the "old members are, so to say, absorbed and assimilated by the newcomers," because the ruling class would then not receive the fresh blood it needs, and instead decline, "turn[ing] to plebs" (ibid.: 425). Mosca concludes that a combination of the two tendencies, the "old doctrine of the golden mean" as he describes it, is the best path, whereas he regards any absolute preponderance of the one tendency over the other as the factor responsible for severe political crises such as those that led, for example, to the end of the Roman Empire or to the Russian Revolution (ibid.: 429).[10]

2.3 The "circulation of elites" (Vilfredo Pareto)

The formulation with which Pareto[11] made his mark in history, including the history of sociology, is his concept of the "circulation of elites" (Pareto 1916 [1935]: § 2042),[12] of the continuous rise and decline of elites. For Pareto, this is an immutable law of history, which no society can elude. Although Pareto's analysis resembles Mosca's in many respects, the context of justification is only partially the same and Pareto's is, above all, much more closely tied into a broad, systematic sociological theory.[13] To begin with, in Chapter 11 of the "Trattato" Pareto quite generally defines elite as a class of people recruited from those who attain the highest levels of achievement in their own field of activity. The kind of activity involved is immaterial for him. He expressly includes both politically powerful or influential persons such as Napoleon or Madame Pompadour and gifted actors, thieves, or even crooks (ibid.: §§ 2032–8).

This view is strongly reminiscent of the functionalist elite theories of later decades, but in the further course of his analysis Pareto is relatively quick to abandon it in favor of a classic dichotomous model. He starts out by subdividing this class of maximum performers into a ruling and a non-ruling elite, the first of which includes all members of the class who "play directly or indirectly a noteworthy role at the highest levels of power" (ibid.: § 2032). The population as a whole, then, Pareto argues, can be broken down into a bipartite elite and the broad mass, the "nonelite lower class" as he at first calls it. A little later he speaks of upper and lower classes, or upper and lower strata, and then of a ruling class, which he equates with the elite. Like Mosca, Pareto is convinced that a small ruling class is to be found everywhere, including in parliamentary democracies, and that it "retains power in part by means of force and in part through the consensus of the ruled class, which may be far larger in size." For Pareto, the notion of "representation of the people" is no more than a "fiction" (ibid.: § 2244).

One decisive factor in Pareto's major objective, an investigation of social equilibrium, is that, in his view, there are "in reality" no exact tests that could be used to come up with a precise assessment of performance and thus to assign every person to his or her correct place. While there are "labels" such as lawyer or minister that serve the same purpose – with or without tests – such labels are unable to prevent unqualified persons from forcing their way into the governing elite. Unlike the case in other fields of human activity where labels have, as a rule, to be obtained by personal means, inheritance, Pareto notes, plays an important role in the case of the ruling elite. This may take on either a direct form (as in the case of many past, and present, monarchies) or an indirect form, as shown by the influence of wealth on the election of senators or members of parliament. If such deviations from the ideal case were insignificant, being of no great import for the development of society, or if they were at least "relatively constant" in terms of their relations, they could be disregarded. This is not the case, however. On the contrary, these deviations, Pareto writes, have considerable influence on social equilibrium (ibid.: §§ 2035–40).

It is at this point that Pareto first speaks of the "circulation of elites," in which either individual persons or, as the case may be, elements of the ruling elite are replaced by upcoming elements from the lower classes, or in which the entire ruling elite is overthrown by a new elite. The crucial factor determining the concrete form of this circulation, Pareto argues, is the intra-elite relationship between those in possession of the traits that enable them to "play an effective part" and those who lack these characteristics. The only way that this process can be accomplished without shaking the foundations of society, Pareto goes on, is for the ruling class to be continuously replenished by persons from the lower classes, with the ruling elite at the same time shedding its "most degenerate members." If, on the other hand, the normal continuity of this circulation were to be tangibly restrained, or even stopped, with the result that superior elements accumulated in the lower strata and inferior elements in the upper strata, this would inevitably lead to the revolutionary overthrow of the ruling class. The extent to which the classes concerned are prepared to use force is a point of particular significance here. If those members of the upper classes who shun the use of force gained the upper hand, and at the same time the lower classes were dominated by those resolved to employ force, the fate of the ruling class would be sealed (ibid.: §§ 2043–59).

The question of force is – and here Pareto introduces into the analysis the categories residues and derivations, which are central to his overall work[14] – determined by the relation between Class I and II residues within both elite and mass, or, in other words, within the upper and lower classes. He defines residues as the immutable emotion-related structures in man which govern the dominant nonlogical part of human actions.[15] Of the six classes of residues, Class I represents the "instinct for combinations," Class II the "persistence of aggregates" (ibid.: §§ 889–1055). The former is responsible for innovations, speculative activities (particularly in the economic sphere), and a certain measure of skepticism, the latter for stable orientations in all areas, that is, for both rentier attitudes in economic life and for fixed systems of values and belief. This, Pareto asserts, can be "compared with inertia in the field of mechanics" (ibid.: § 992). Over time, however, the Class II residues tend to weaken in the upper classes, i.e. their religious feelings, their propensity to save, and their willingness to use force.

In Chapter 12, in particular, Pareto looks in more depth into the connection between residues and the circulation of elites (ibid.: §§ 2178–392). His argument is based on the assumption that a ruling class will frequently attempt to prevent or overcome any violent opposition by "cunning, deception, and bribery." This behavior, commensurate with the task of ruling, provides in the long run for a marked shift in favor of Class I residues as opposed to Class II residues. The "foxes," Pareto notes, following Machiavelli, have ousted the "lions" (ibid.: § 2178). On a political plane, he goes on, this means that long-term intangible interests are replaced by short-term materialistic interests; in economic terms this implies that cautious rentiers will be replaced by adventuresome and innovative speculators; and in ideological terms it means that belief in ideals will be replaced by scientific skepticism.

Pareto notes that these changes initially have wholly positive consequences on the efforts of the ruling class to sustain its power. A tactical and expedient approach in politics, he notes, initially goes some way toward stabilizing its position. This applies in particular when the ruling class succeeds in absorbing the majority of those people among the ruled masses who possess the "instinct for combinations." In this way the "governed class" would be deprived of its potential leaders and rendered incapable of "initiating anything of a durable nature" (ibid.: § 2179). In the economy, Pareto writes, there is good reason to assess the strengthening of innovative, speculative elements in a similar vein. Admittedly, he goes on, they would bring "into the ruling class many people who would destroy wealth, but also many more who would create it," as the economic prosperity of the civilized Western nations has very clearly shown (ibid.: § 2301). Strong economic growth, Pareto asserts, is a central prerequisite for those governments that renounce the use of force and turn instead to cunning, deceit, or (in general terms) tactical behaviors. On the one hand, he continues, they need constant growth for their short-term public debt policies, and on the other hand they are far more vulnerable to economic crises than governments that rely mainly on force.

The potential dangers that are, in Pareto's view, involved in the displacement of Class II residues are already in evidence here. Pareto contends that, in the long run, the positive traits mentioned above will not be able to prevent the power of the ruling elite from being threatened and eventually broken, with a new elite replacing the old. The main factor involved here is the unwillingness of the ruling class to resort to the use of force. With the continuous decline of the elements in possession of residues of persistence, the class gradually declines and eventually vanishes more or less completely. Pareto expands on this in Chapter 13, where he argues that in contemporary society the principle reason for this decline is the fact that the ruling class impedes, or indeed even prevents, the normal circulation of elites. If the ruling class reaches a point where it only accepts elements of the governed class that aspire to resemble the members of the ruling class, often, "with the ardor" of the newly converted, even overshooting the goal, this will, in tendency, serve to further strengthen the abundant residues of combination already at hand in the ruling class instead of weakening them, as would in fact be required (ibid.: §§ 2482–5). On the other hand, the lower classes will display more and more elements marked by very strong residues of persistence, and these elements "know how to use force." They, Pareto claims, replace the old and constitute a new elite, the entire cycle starts anew, "and so forth" (ibid.: § 2319).

Revolutions hence always break out when the discrepancy between the increase in instincts for combination in the ruling class and the growth of the persistence of aggregates in the governed class becomes "sufficiently large" (ibid.: § 2179).[16] In addition to a willingness to use force, the decrease in Class II residues among the governing class also results in a decline in the belief in common ideals. The skepticism burgeoning within this class not only weakens its powers of resistance, it also favors the emergence of humanitarian sentiments in its ranks. Elements particularly affected by this development may then even go over to the side of the governed class, providing the lower class with the leaders it lacks. While, Pareto argues, the latter does develop elements that are in possession of the "residues needed to rule" and are "resolved to use force," revolutions are nevertheless generally led "by people from the upper classes, because it is these persons who [possess] the intellectual skills needed for this struggle" (ibid.: § 2058).

2.4 The "iron law of oligarchy" (Robert Michels)

In the most important (and today by far best-known) of his books, *Political Parties. A Sociological Study of the Oligarchic Tendencies of Modern Democracy*,[17] Robert Michels,[18] the third of our classic analysts of the sociology of elites, pursues an approach less comprehensive than that of Mosca and Pareto. While the intention of Mosca and Pareto was, as the titles of their major works indicate, to develop a set of universal principles for the fields of political science and sociology, Michels' major concern is with an analysis of modern political parties. His principle interest was the question of intraparty democracy, an issue which he investigated using German Social Democracy as his prime example, since, as he noted, social-revolutionary parties such as the SPD see as their "principle aim the struggle against oligarchy in all its forms." The emergence of oligarchic tendencies in such parties is, he goes on, therefore of particular significance and "proof of the existence of immanent oligarchic tendencies in every kind of human organization which strives for the attainment of definite ends" (Michels 1911: 12). In the introduction to his study Michels states clearly that he views such tendencies as an inevitable and basic principle of any party organization. In an explicit reference to Mosca – and here he goes far beyond the immediate field of political parties – he even speaks of an inevitable contradiction in all emancipation movements. These, like humanity in general, are said to be unable to dispense with the "political class," even though this class inevitably constitutes only a "fraction" of society (ibid.: 20).

Michels begins his actual analysis, however, with a statement which places organization in a positive light. Without organization, he asserts, democracy is inconceivable. This, he claims, is the only way in which the working class can develop political resistance, for as an individual the proletarian is the weakest link in society and as such "defenseless in the hands of those who are economically more powerful." He does, however, immediately go on to restrict this assessment. At the same time, he notes, the principle of organization implicitly contains all those dangers which disfigure democracy, sometimes even rendering it "unrecognizable" (ibid.: 21–2). "With the advance of organization, democracy tends to decline" (ibid.: 33).

In what follows, Michel cites three causes which he sees as responsible for the inevitable oligarchization of instrumental human organizations. He breaks these causes down into technical-administrative, psychological, and intellectual factors. In technical-administrative terms, oligarchic tendencies are chiefly promoted by the fact that a "direct self-administration" consonant with the ideals of democracy is technically impossible due to the large numbers of people involved. This applies for public and party assemblies alike. If these are to be capable of taking action, he notes, they are forced to elect delegates and a leadership. However, all attempts to subject this leadership to direct democratic control are ultimately doomed to failure, simply because the sheer size of the organization renders this impossible. Growing internal differentiation tends in the same direction. A "strong organization," Michels notes in summary, gives rise to a "strong leadership," i.e. to professional leaders. This, however, means "the beginning of the end of democracy" (ibid.: 35–6).

In the considerably more in-depth analysis of psychological causes which follows, Michels' argumentation and formulations are strongly reminiscent of Le Bon. According to this view, the crucial factor involved here is the unwillingness of the broad masses to deal with the issues arising from the problems facing the organization. The majority is happy to be able to find people to whom they can delegate such tasks. The "need for leadership" implied here is bound up with both the inability of the masses to take the initiative and, for the most part, also with "worship" of leaders, who are regarded as "heroes." For Michels, the "inherent weakness" of the masses is demonstrated by the fact that they behave like a confused anthill, or indeed "take flight in chaotic disorder" when they have lost their leaders in action (ibid.: 53–5). The masses are not only grateful to their leaders for the sacrifices they have made in the past, they also revere them. "In their primitive idealism" they need "worldly gods" (ibid.: 67). The third and decisive cause, Michels contends, is that this passive attitude is reinforced by the intellectual superiority of the professional leadership, which is a result primarily of practical experience gained in party work. The gulf between leadership and masses continues to grow as a function of the increasing need for specialized knowledge. This goes for parliamentary work in particular. Ultimately, it is the "incompetence of the mass" which constitutes the "most solid foundation of the power of the leaders" (ibid.: 83).

The leaders, with their power enormously strengthened by the factors mentioned above, are then, thanks to various developments, able to stabilize and consolidate this power. Initially, the "law of inertia," a mixture of traditional sentiment and a desire for stable conditions on the part of the masses, favors the repeated reelection of those once elected to top leadership positions (ibid.: 93). Added to this, Michels goes on, is the growing tendency of these leaders to fill their own ranks by means of cooptation (ibid.: 99–101), to exert their financial power over party functionaries, whom they make use of to "consolidate and secure" their own power (ibid.: 123), and to harness the press to their own ends. Thus, with the "constitution of leadership," Michels argues, begins "its transformation into a closed caste" (ibid.: 151). Not even the continuous emergence of oppositional forces can change this tendency, he notes. The opposition is either, as is generally the case, coopted by the established party leadership's conferral of posts and honors, thus leading to an "amalgamation of the two" (ibid.: 184–5), or – a rare case – the opposition does in fact gain the day, but only then to alter its character to such an extent that it is ultimately indistinguishable from the old leaders. The "revolutionaries of the present," thus Michels' suggestive conclusion, are the "reactionaries of the future" (ibid.: 191–3).

Michels then goes on to look in detail at the psychological changes to which party leaders are subject once they have been elected. He observes a "natural hunger for power" among such leaders. Those in power will, as a rule, attempt to extend their power and to elude the control of the masses (ibid.: 195). Possession of power inevitably affects character. This is particularly true when the concern is to gain a share of "public power" (ibid.: 201). An additional factor at work here is material dependence on a party, since neither former workers nor "defectors from the bourgeoisie" are in a position to return to their old professions (ibid.: 196–7). In the long term, furthermore, it is inevitable that leaders come to regard themselves as an "expression of the general will of the masses" (ibid.: 209) and increasingly equate the party with their own person (ibid.: 215–17).

Michels devotes the final part of his book to an attempt to draw some general conclusions from his analysis of the modern system of political parties. Here he refers explicitly to core propositions of Mosca and Pareto. Although his formulations are not always entirely unambiguous, since he refers to the two other theorists in the indicative mood, which makes it impossible to distinguish between what he is reporting and the position he himself holds, many central points show clear signs of substantive agreement; the wording chosen for the chapter heading, the "iron law of oligarchy," is characteristic in this respect. Michels then, however, goes beyond his basic thesis that every organization is bound to develop oligarchies, a process which he regards as "organic" in nature (ibid.: 385). Here he provides no more than general observations on the possibility of democratic rule in a given society.

In the end Michels comes to the same conclusions as Mosca and Pareto. Putting his position in a nutshell, he notes tersely that "leadership is a necessary concomitant of every form of social life" (ibid.: 383). The "factual immaturity of the masses" is rooted in the "amorphous nature of the mass itself, which, though organized, is immanently incompetent when faced with the complex of tasks it has to deal with, because it is in need of division of labor, specialization, and guidance" (ibid.: 338). The struggles between aristocracy and democracy or between government and opposition are, Michels remarks, no more than struggles between a minority which is already in power but which wishes to monopolize its rule[19] and a minority which seeks to gain power. This process does not even lead to a replacement of the old by a new minority, and the outcome is merely an amalgamation of the two. One "clique of the ruling class" is simply replaced by another. It is, Michels claims, in this sense that even the French revolution was unable to really oust the aristocracy from power (ibid.: 363–5).

Finally, Michels summarizes the results of his analysis in the "the principle that one dominant class inevitably succeeds to another, and the law deduced from that principle that oligarchy is, as it were, a preordained form of the common life of great social aggregates" (ibid.: 376). Despite this pessimistic stance Michels does not consider the democratic principle to be fundamentally wrong. In his final remarks Michels notes that the democratic principle offers at least the chance of a certain "mitigation of the oligarchic disease," since it is the essence of democracy, and the workers' movement, to strengthen the individual's ability to criticize and control. Compared with the aristocracy, then, democracy must always be seen as the "lesser evil" (ibid.: 389–91).[20]

2.5 Summary

The theoretical approaches pursued by three classic authors of the sociology of elites show a good measure of agreement in their core propositions, though with some important differences. What is common to all three is on the one hand their fundamental subdivision of society into elite and mass and on the other their use of the figure of the circulation of elites.

In the contrast between elite and mass the three authors see a universally valid principle of the history of mankind. In their view the great mass is at all times, irrespective of development epoch and form of government, ruled over by a small elite using various means to the end (force being one of the principle among them). The elite is in possession of the material, intellectual, and psychological capacities required to exercise power, and thus to rule, while the mass is without them. The mass is not only intellectually inferior and ruled by its emotions, it is at the same time, and in a dual sense, in want of leadership, in both subjective and objective terms.

However, a closer look also shows some marked differences beneath this general assessment. Pareto, for example, is the only one of the three to attempt systematically to develop a universal definition of the concept "elite." In using his core concept "ruling class," Mosca largely restricts his observations to a wide variety of historical examples (mostly from ancient, but also more modern European history) to elucidate what he has in mind. Finally, while Michels, focusing on German social democracy, deals in great detail with the issue of leadership and rank and file, his general conclusions wholly lack a clear definition of the concepts used and make use instead of the terminology developed by Mosca and Pareto. One point which unites the three again is their constant alternation between various terms such as elite, ruling class, governing class, political class, upper class, aristocracy, or upper classes on the one hand and mass, masses, ruled class, lower class, or lower classes on the other. This not only demonstrates that Pareto by no means succeeds in his attempt to stick to a strict definition, it also shows how unsystematically, indeed at times how unreflectedly, superficially, and arbitrarily, all three classic theorists operate with key concepts.[21] The question of the relation between elites and classes, which is of central relevance to the sociology of elites, remains totally unresolved in this connection.

Against this background it is not surprising that, as far as both Mosca and Pareto are concerned, considerable substantive uncertainties remain and many questions are left unanswered. This is particularly evident where they endeavor to draw distinctions within the elite. Mosca, for example, in his chapter dealing with "Evolution of Political Organization," states expressly that below "the highest stratum in the ruling class" there is always "another that is much more numerous and comprises all the capacities for leadership" (Mosca 1896 [1939]: 404). It is on this class, and not on the uppermost class of society, that the stability of every polity ultimately depends. Mosca cites as examples the officers corps below the level of the general staff as well as top-level civil servants, that is, groups which, in the language he has used up to this point, can unquestionably be regarded as belonging to the ruling class. The impression he makes with this point is then counteracted only two pages later by his formulation that bureaucrats are "in fact always recruited from the middle classes, in other words from the second stratum of the ruling class" (ibid.: 408). If at this point Mosca designates the overall middle classes as the lower stratum of the ruling class, in doing so he is dramatically enlarging the concept of the ruling class, but without drawing the consequences for his overall analysis.

Pareto's case is similar. He divides the elite into a ruling and a nonruling group. What he means by the latter, however, remains somewhat nebulous. Immediately after making this distinction Pareto defines the latter as those members of the elite who (like famous chess players, for example) are at the top in their own field, but who neither directly nor indirectly "play a notable role at the highest levels of power" (Pareto 1916 [1935]: §§ 2032–4). However, he then immediately abandons this definition, either no longer mentioning this group or populating it with other groupings such as politicians. Yet in the next chapter it is precisely these politicians that he describes as "people of the ruled class," people who are used by the ruling class as one of the two principle instruments to shore up its power, namely as policemen or soldiers or as politicians (ibid.: § 2257). Pareto, then, is no closer to providing a precise definition than Mosca is.

A closer look at the central argumentation of the "circulation of elites" presents a similarly unclear picture. The basic pattern is relatively clear at the outset: there is a regular and continuous exchange within the ruling class or elite, and, above all, between the latter and the ruled class or mass. The former can only continue to assert its power in the long run if it succeeds in absorbing the most qualified elements of the latter. In the course of time, however, this process is increasingly checked or even halted by efforts of the ruling class to "hereditarize" their positions, and thus to monopolize them. For Pareto, there comes a point at which the barriers so restrict the access of the required "new blood" that the normal circulation no longer functions and revolutions break out, in the course of which the old ruling class is replaced by a new one.

Yet the three classic theorists share this basic figure in its core only, and on one crucial issue Michels' position clearly differs from the others. In contrast to Mosca and Pareto, he denies that the old ruling class is in fact replaced, even in revolutions; instead, he sees a permanent amalgamation of old elites with new, upcoming elements (Michels 1911: 364). This difference points to the basic weakness of the circulation model, which remains strangely anemic and abstract despite the numerous historical examples cited. It lacks any real foundation.

This applies for Pareto in particular. In explaining the circulation of elites essentially with reference to changes in the composition of the residues in the ruling and the ruled class, this – principally psychological – justification leads him into two major dilemmas. First, he is unable to show conclusively why the residues of the elite and the mass change in the manner he describes, and second, he provides no answer to the question why the normal circulation does not function on a permanent basis, why revolutions are inevitable at one point or another. In any case, his major line of argument is anything but cogent. Efforts of the ruling class to monopolize its position, and the blockades to advancement which these entail, are clearly not sufficient to set revolutionary processes in motion, as Bottomore illustrates with reference to India, with its very rigid caste structure (Bottomore 1993

[1963]: 39). Accordingly, Pareto's premise that revolutions inevitably break out when there is a "sufficiently large" disparity between residues must be seen as overly general and lacking in concrete substance.

Without going into real, in particular sociostructural changes, this line of argumentation is bound to remain largely formal and ahistorical. This also applies in essence for Mosca, even though he does pay considerably more attention to the material conditions required for processes of change. To a far greater degree than Pareto, he points to the important role played by social influences in shaping the psychological characteristics of the ruling class, and he also sees social forces playing a far larger role in the circulation of the ruling classes. Despite these differences, Mosca (like Pareto and Michels) sees history basically as a constantly recurring cycle in which the one ruling class or elite replaces the other. The Enlightenment's optimistic view of mankind and its development potentials gives way in all three authors to a pessimistic stance. In their eyes human history has only one pattern: small minorities unceasingly struggling for power, while the broad majority of the population more or less looks passively on. Michels provides the most dramatic formulation: "The masses are content to employ all their strength to change masters" (Michels 1911: 377).

Although their ideological, and in part their practical, proximity to Italian fascism brought the works of Mosca, Pareto, and Michels into disrepute for many years after the end of the Second World War,[22] their influence on the sociology of elites or, indeed on the research and discussion on elites in general, remains unbroken to this day. With his attempt to develop an equilibrium model of society, and in his abstract definition of the concept of elite, Pareto may even be seen as a direct precursor of the functionalist theories of elites which, since the 1950s, superseded the classic view and which is today still dominant in the debate on elites.

Questions

1   How does Le Bon characterize the mass?
2   What does Mosca understand by the ruling class's effort of monopolization?
3   What's the meaning of the "circulation of elites" in Pareto?
4   Which reasons does Michels give for the "iron law of oligarchy"?

3   Functional elites

In view of the experience of Italian and – above all – of German fascism, the Machiavellian elite theories of Michels, Mosca, and Pareto, with their ideological (and indeed in part even personal) affinity to this system of rule, were viewed very critically after the end of the Second World War both by the general public and by the academic world. In the eyes of the large majority the crimes of fascism had utterly discredited the basic view held by the classic elite sociologists that the great majority was bound to be ruled by a small minority. The term elite now came to be associated first and foremost with the racial delusions of the National Socialists and the murder of millions of supposedly racially inferior Jews and Slavs to which this led, but also with the Fuehrer principle in politics and society, with the Nazis' elite schools, with the SS "Lebensborn" program, the goal of which was to breed "racially valuable human material," and so on. All these forms of fascism were associated with one central idea – the superiority of a chosen minority – an idea which immediately brought the theories of Michels, Mosca, and Pareto to mind.

3.1 Mass and functional elites

The debate over fascism and its devastating consequences posed a key problem for research on elites. How could the relation between elite and mass be redefined without falling back into the old, classic dichotomy? Most social scientists saw, and still see today, the solution in theoretical approaches focusing on pluralist functional elites.

The first well-known sociologist to argue along these lines was Karl Mannheim.[1] In the first version of his study *Man and Society in an Age of Reconstruction*, which appeared in 1935, Mannheim, in the section on "the social causes of the present cultural crisis," spoke explicitly not only of various types of elite but also of an "accumulation of elite groups" and the emergence of the meritocratic principle as the key factor in the selection of elites. The basic elements of this distinction bear considerable likeness to the functionalist theories of elites which became dominant in the fifties, although more or less clear-cut differences can be discerned in the lines of argument presented here and there.

Mannheim distinguishes three types of elite: political and organizational elites, intellectual and artistic elites, and moral and religious elites. He sees the first two types principally in business, administration, and politics, where they are responsible for the integration of the "various volitions." The task of the other four is "to spiritualize mental energies," that is to say, to develop and unfold a nation's science and culture (Mannheim 1935 [1967]: 96). Both types of elite are assumed to be indispensable for a society. Mass society, which is basically open and democratic, is now assumed to ensure the growth of both the number and the size of elite groups. The result of this is that, first, these groups become less exclusive and second, that the third of the three major principles of selection in operation in the history of mankind – birth, property, and performance – gradually assume predominance, more and more frequently becoming the sole criterion of selection (ibid.: 100–13).

Although for Mannheim these changes are on the one hand essential for the continued development of society, they also represent a great danger, primarily to culture. Initially, for instance, the growth in elite groups has a stimulating effect in breaking up the rigidity and closed character of earlier small elites, but "beyond a certain limit" this "multiplicity" turns into "haziness," and individual elites begin to neutralize one another, with the result that none of them are any longer able to shape society as a whole. The loss of exclusivity which this implies prevents the development of a leading taste or principle of style, and the outcome is a constant hunger for fleeting stimuli and a general lack of orientation (ibid). This effect is reinforced by the destruction of the intermediary structures that once served to mediate between elites and masses. In mass society a constant general public, made up of estate-like strata, is replaced by an "occasional" public that is far more subject to the laws of mass psychology and tends primarily to react to sensations. A similar process, Mannheim notes, can be observed in politics, where constancy is also vanishing and the irrationality of the masses is gaining more and more weight (ibid.: 114–15).

Mannheim sees comparable dangers as regards the preponderance of the performance principle. This principle is crucial as a dynamic element of social development; yet it not only harbors the risk of depriving society of the continuity it needs, worse still, "mass society" is threatened with degeneration "into fascism" if it lacks objective performance criteria and equitable principles of social selection (ibid.: 107–8). At a later stage Mannheim supplements this point by arguing that precisely the "democratization of social advancement through education" entails a decisive negative consequence, the "proletarization of the intelligentsia," and with it a devaluation of cultural and intellectual work in the public sphere. While this detachment of the intelligentsia from "good society" initially led to a flourishing of culture and science, in the long run it undermines their foundations in that the "more limited intelligence of the average person" tends to gain more and more weight, finally becoming the universal paradigm. Mannheim sees lower middle-class elements as playing the main role in this process, hankering as they do for purely material reasons, after preindustrial times, and in this way generating intellectual regression (ibid.: 120ff).

As this last argument shows, Mannheim assembles three different viewpoints in his analysis. Many of his lines of thought take up Le Bon's ideas on mass psychology and Pareto and Mosca's elite-mass model; others (for instance, his assessment of the petty bourgeoisie) clearly have recourse to a Marxist class analysis; and yet others bear clear indications of a functionalist viewpoint. It is in this respect that Mannheim differs clearly from the pioneer of American research on elites, Harold D. Lasswell,[2] whose books *World Politics and Personal Insecurity* (1934) and *Politics: Who Gets What, When and How* (1936) reveal the pronounced influence of Pareto. Lasswell not only follows Pareto in his clear contrasting of elite and mass, he also, like Pareto, concentrates primarily on the psychological conditions required to capture and hold positions of power, nearly wholly neglecting sociostructural processes.[3] He argues that in order to secure their power, elites must above all be able to manipulate the masses with all the means at their disposal, including symbols, force, or material goods.

Even though Pareto's influence wanes somewhat in Lasswell's later works, and although Pareto had considerably less impact on other representatives of US elite research, Lasswell's early approach remains characteristic in two ways for the majority of studies on the subject of elites published in the US during the first two post-war decades.[4] There are two aspects that characterize these studies: first, the fact that they neglect or even discount entirely strata and class structures and the social processes associated with them, and second, their highly critical attitude toward the masses, which, in its basic traits, is reminiscent of both the three classic theorists and of Karl Mannheim.[5]

One typical example of this latter approach is William Kornhauser, who, in his analysis *The Politics of Mass Society* (1959), sees democracy as threatened not by ruling elites but by the masses and the counterelites to which they give rise. He contends that it is only the established elites that have an interest in the stability of the dominant democratic order and that it is only internal competition among the various subelites that prevent them from abusing their power. The masses and the counterelites are not bound in the same way to this order and its values, and in view of their susceptibility to populist ideals and efforts at mobilization, they thus represent a real danger for the democratic system. Kornhauser goes on to argue that a system in which there is easy access to elites generates pressure on the part of the masses which then prevents elites "from performing their creative and value-sustaining functions" (ibid.: 28). It is important to counter any direct influence on the part of the masses because the masses inhibit or even prevent the elites from autonomously addressing the tasks at hand, a state of affairs that calls for so-called "mid-elites" (specialists like lawyers) that form a buffer between elites and nonelites (ibid.: 99). In their book *Power and Society*, which appeared in 1950, Lasswell and Kaplan are more explicit. They state expressly that "whatever increases the power potential of the mass will tend also to shift allocation in the direction of autocracy" (Lasswell and Kaplan 1950: 221).

The lines of argument presented by Kornhauser and also Lasswell and Kaplan are symptomatic of the mainstream US discussion on elites in the 1950s. They express, on the one hand, a deeply rooted mistrust of the general population. On the other hand, they see democratic power relations as safeguarded by the existence not of a single, uniform elite but of a number of competing subelites from various spheres of society whose power is restricted by the power wielded by the other subelites.[6] Chances to wield influence on political decisions or overall social developments, which depend in large measure on property, income, profession, education, etc., do not for this reason pose a major problem for most such authors. In their view there are only two principle requirements for a functioning democracy. There must be effective competition among the established subelites, and at the same time these elites must be generally accessible to the masses.

Lasswell and Kaplan state this quite clearly. Having noted that depending on its effectiveness, political equality gives rise to corresponding degrees of social and economic equality, they go on to define this political equality not as equal distribution of power but as equal distribution of "access to power." Thus political equality is "a matter of equal eligibility to power status" (ibid.: 226–7). The concept "eligibility" shows that they (like, incidentally, the large majority of sociologists and political scientists involved in the debate) concentrate primarily on politics in the narrower sense of the term, largely ignoring the distribution of power in other areas such as business. It would not be so easy to make "eligibility" the key criterion here and then to come up with a positive response. This reservation applies as well for less conservative social scientists such as Robert Dahl.[7] While in his well-known study on the power structures in the town of New Haven, Connecticut, Dahl does not restrict himself to a discussion of politicians, in looking into debates concerning selection of party candidates, development of public education systems, and urban planning he does confine his investigation largely to the immediate political decision-making structures involved. Typically, Dahl's investigation focuses on New Haven's mayor – rather than the town's social and business elite, which he sees as divided – and the mayor is cast in the role of the driving force behind the town's urban renewal program.[8]

But what clearly distinguishes Dahl from Lasswell is the former's far more critical view of the issue of chances of access. True, the study describes what Dahl sees as the central historical development of what initially was a largely homogeneous elite into a socially and ethnically mixed, pluralist elite, but he also points out that even today the chances individuals have of participating in political decision-making processes grow in proportion to the resources – income, education, profession, etc. – available to them (Dahl

1961: 282–3). From this he derives, at another point in the study, his demand for true equality of opportunity where "each adult citizen should have an equal and indefinitely enduring opportunity to exercise as much power over key government decisions as any other citizen exercises" (Dahl 1964: 17; quoted in Bachrach 1966: 89). For Dahl, this demand would be met only if recruitment to political positions took place in a manner ensuring proportional representation of class, race, gender, etc., based on the share of these groups in society as a whole. In this respect, as in his skeptical assessment of the chances of democratic participation, Dahl remains an exception.[9] The vast majority of US social scientists dealing with elites hold a markedly positive view of the existing parliamentary system and its elites.

3.2 Functional elites and democracy

Although, generally speaking, the German elite research (with its most well-known representatives, Dahrendorf, Dreitzel, Stammer, and Zapf) conducted in the two post-war decades both shares this positive assessment and subscribes to the functionalist approach to elites, it differs in two important respects from the thrust of the studies published at the same time in the US. First, German research does not disregard the link between elites and social or class structure; on the contrary, this is one of its core focuses of interest,[10] as is unmistakably indicated for example by the title of Dreitzel's central work, *Elitebegriff und Sozialstruktur/Social Structure and the Concept of Elite* (1962). Second, this research direction is not marked by a fundamentally negative attitude toward the masses, and elites are subjected to a far more critical examination.

Basically, both these points are associated with the fact that Pareto's theory of elites, the direct and indirect influence of which was highly evident in the US even after the Second World War, was openly rejected and criticized by the most important representatives of German elite research. To cite an example: In a 1951 article on the "Elite Problem in Democracy," Stammer[11] expressly criticizes the "anti-democratic tendency" in the works of Mosca and Pareto, who, he argues, have, "without doubt had a very powerful influence on the political and ideological practice of elite formation in various totalitarian systems" (Stammer 1965a: 68).[12] As his most clear-cut example, he cites the "intellectual world and practice" of National Socialism. There is little doubt that his and Dahrendorf's[13] personal experience of the demise of the Weimar Republic, and subsequently with the National Socialist regime, played a decisive role in their rejection of the classic theories of elites.

Both authors were able to observe at close hand the role of the traditional German elites during the breakup of the Weimar Republic and the rise of the Nazis, and both were later persecuted by the Nazis for their political views and activities. Dahrendorf, son of a Social Democrat member of the Reichstag, was arrested in 1944 for "activities endangering the state";

Stammer, an active member of the SPD, was forbidden either to publish or to work in his profession during the Nazi period. It is thus not surprising that Stammer saw the key reason for the failure of the Weimar Republic not in the immaturity or insufficient political quality of the working class or the "popular masses" but first and foremost in "the mistakes it made in elite formation." The elites of the Weimar Republic, he contends, had lost their effectiveness because their tendency to form isolated but privileged groups meant they were no longer able to establish the necessary link between the population and the national government. The latter was in this way deprived of its "most important political tool in the defense of democracy" (ibid.: 79–81).

Although Stammer's criticism of the closure of elites is reminiscent of the theories of Michels, Mosca, and Pareto, in his arguments he explicitly criticizes their theory of a universal oligarchization of elites. For him, this proposition is justified with respect to undemocratic systems, but not with respect to democratic systems. In democratic systems, he contends, the social and political competition between individual elites and their obligation to justify themselves and be held accountable for their actions by their "mother groups" as well as by the people ensured that the existing psychological tendency toward isolation did not as a rule come to bear (ibid.: 82).

It is here that Stammer's fundamental theoretical position on the question of elites takes on clear shape. What he means by elites under the conditions of democratic mass society is, first, socially or politically influential groups from a variety of areas that arise from the population by way of delegation or competition and assume a given function in the system and, second, groups which take on certain political leadership functions. These groups are all on a footing of mutual competition. Their primary role is that of a "functional intermediary" between the people and the government (ibid.: 71). Stammer asserts that only these groups are able to guarantee the functioning of mass democracy, not only because "the selection of the state's top leaders lies entirely in their hands" but also because only they are in a position to ensure that the masses are able to control these leaders and, conversely, to successfully convey the latter's decisions to the masses (ibid.: 77).

These elites are, in principle, open and include, in Stammer's analysis, leading groups of the state apparatus (government bodies and parliamentary factions, sections of ministerial bureaucracy, justice, and the army), leading members of parties and associations, or representatives of capital interests, large corporations, and the labor unions. Access to these elites, and thus a certain measure of participation in leadership, is open to everyone able and willing to "take on a particular function in the dominant sociopolitical structure and to deliver the performance expected of this function." It is only such performance-linked competition that guarantees the ability of elites, and indeed of the democratic system as a whole, to function. In contrast to the ruling classes of the past, the leading stratum of democratic mass society is thus no longer "an upper social class or aristocracy" or a closed and privileged group defined in terms of family, property, or education. On the contrary, it functions "on behalf of and under the control of" the people (Stammer 1965b: 177).[14]

Stammer sees the greatest weakness in and hence threat to this system in the fact that elites are coordinated in processes of give and take among the mother groups; he notes that the resulting competition can, in extreme cases, reach a stage at which the necessary levels of technical cooperation are no longer assured (Stammer 1965a: 89). For him it is therefore essential for a sociological analysis of elites to obtain a clear view of their mother groups and, ultimately, of the social classes behind them. It is only possible to analyze the rise and the functions of elites by paying due heed to "their relationship to the overall social structure" (Stammer 1965a: 85; 1965b: 171).

Dahrendorf shares this basic premise. In his theoretical approach, which sees social conflict as the driving force behind social development,[15] classes play even a greater role than they do in Stammer's approach. However, this aspect bears little fruit in Dahrendorf's work on elites, since he fails to work out any precise terminological definitions. Dahrendorf does move from his preference for the term upper classes in his early publications to the terms elite and ruling groups in his later works, but he does not proceed systematically in this respect. In 1961 he speaks, in "Society and Freedom," of functional elites, but then simply classifies them as part of the upper classes. In his essay "A new German upper class?" he distinguishes between the prestige upper class, the economic upper class, and the ruling class or power elite as the three crucial leadership groups and points out that the composition of these three groups can, but need not, overlap. But then he goes on, one page later, to blur the analytical potentials resulting from this distinction by undifferentiatedly classifying all three groups as elites (Dahrendorf 1972: 126–36).[16]

Despite this lack of terminological focus, Dahrendorf's basic patterns of argumentation remain the same. In his view there is no longer a unified upper class but simply a multitude of competing leadership groups or functional elites. At one point he even speaks of "competing sub-upper classes" (Dahrendorf 1961: 179). Even though in essence he is referring to one and the same thing, Dahrendorf does differentiate in specifically classifying these groups: he speaks initially of seven functional elites corresponding to the "great institutional orders" of society – the economy, politics, education, religion, culture, the military, and law (Dahrendorf 1961: 179), in order later to cite only four categories – the holders of formal positions of power, formal administrative positions with political power, other positions with political power (e.g. in associations), and other positions with political influence (e.g. the heads of large corporations or labor unions (Dahrendorf 1972: 127).

His intention is to prove that notions of a unified power elite or upper class no longer adequately reflect the conditions given in modern industrial society. High income does not necessarily, as he puts it in 1961, secure great power, and such power does not necessarily mean high prestige (Dahrendorf 1961: 178). In the same way, he asserts, the sizable overlaps between the groups of the economic upper classes and the power elite do nothing to alter the principle difference between the two groups or the competition between the economic upper classes and other groups that "may at times lose out, but may at other times succeed" when the power elite has important decisions to make (Dahrendorf 1962: 30).

Over and above this, Dahrendorf develops a very general model to characterize elites based on two criteria: social status and stature on the one hand and political interests and attitude on the other. If an elite displays a high degree of social homogeneity (birth or descent, education, professional position, etc.), he speaks of an established elite, whereas his term for an elite lacking commonalities and concerned not with "real phenomena" but with the "phenomena of order" constructed by sociologists is abstract elite. As far as concrete interests are concerned, Dahrendorf distinguishes between a uniform position, in which interests and ideas are largely consistent, and a multiform position, in which interests and ideas tend to vary, indeed even to be contradictory. From this state of affairs he then derives four basic types of elite: authoritarian (established and uniform), totalitarian (abstract and uniform), liberal (established and multiform), and an unspecified type which is abstract in its social embodiment and multiform in its political attitude (Dahrendorf 1965: 257–9). While, initially, Dahrendorf shows an unmistakable preference for the third type, which is quite obviously coined for the traditional British elite as a positive counterexample to the German situation, and indeed even regards the "established elite" as the sine qua non for the continued existence of a free and democratic constitution of society, he then goes on to speak unambiguously of the abstract elite, viewed in the light of the fourth type, as the "ruling class of the future." There will, he argues, no longer be any "truly coherent classes" but only "fearful rulers, divided among themselves, uncertain as to their position" (Dahrendorf 1972: 136).[17]

As far as the Dahrendorf's terminological system is concerned, it must be said that Dreitzel[18] is the exact opposite of Dahrendorf. In this respect Dreitzel's analysis of the concept elite remains exemplary to this day, arguably surpassed only by Suzanne Keller's *Beyond the Ruling Class*. Dreitzel's argumentation is rooted in the basic premise that democratic industrial society is based on a continuous increase in productivity and standards of living and that its hierarchical structure thus centers on performance-related qualification rather than on possession of capital, as was the case in the bourgeois class society typical of the nineteenth century. The complex functional relationships in a democratic industrial society, he notes, are inevitably based on a specialization which rewards "technical performance alone." Meritocratic qualification has, in his eyes, replaced capital as the key factor of production. As a result, not only has class antagonism lost its significance but this has also led to a "multiplication of elites" (Dreitzel 1962: 49–56, 73, 79, 155).

Thus, for Dreitzel, the elite includes all those who have attained top positions as a result of a performance-based selection process; this might, in theory, obtain for every sphere of personal achievement, although ultimately it includes only those areas which are of interest and significance for society. In this regard, Dreitzel argues, performance-based qualification is a necessary but not sufficient condition. Success in the sense of a public acknowledgment of concrete performance is also necessary. Dreitzel sums up his definition of elite as follows:

> An elite is made up of the holders of top positions in a group, organization, or institution who have acceded to these positions on the basis of a selection process geared primarily to their (personal) performance-based knowledge and who have, thanks to their role in this position, the power or the influence needed to contribute directly, and beyond the immediate interests of their own group, to maintaining or changing the social structure or the norms that sustain it, or those whose prestige places them in a position to play an exemplary role that has a normative function in determining the behavior of other persons over and above their own group.
>
> (Dreitzel 1962: 71)

This meritocratic selection process which governs access to elites, Dreitzel argues, is, in essence, institutionalized in the form of a professional structure and the schooling and professional training which precedes it. In principle, it is possible for anyone to acquire the educational or vocational qualifications conferred here, and hence to advance into elite positions. Dreitzel attaches great importance to pointing out that these opportunities are only open in principle, and not in fact, to everyone, and he is fully aware of the existing inequalities of opportunity in education and the professional world. In his view, however, these are the result primarily of strata-specific educational and status goals, and they therefore cast no doubt on the principle of meritocratic selection for elite positions, even though they do significantly restrict vertical mobility (ibid.: 110–11).[19] Consequently, democratic industrial society as a whole may, in his eyes, be characterized as an elite society in which selection for elite positions is based on performance and in which these positions are in principle open to all citizens.

Dreitzel frequently stresses, however, that, defined in this way, the "elitist social structure" is an ideal type that, in this form, does not prevail in reality. In his view, the term "elite society" does not necessarily mean that all top positions are filled exclusively on the basis of performance criteria but merely that society shows an increasing tendency to proceed in this way[20] (ibid.: 72–3). There are, in his opinion, two important factors which place limits on pure meritocracy. First, meritocracy is a "utopia" inasmuch as success, in addition to achievement, is inevitably required for access to elites and "no success is based purely on objective performance" (ibid.: 99).

Instead, success always presupposes the ability to assert one's own interests. In order to make a success out of one's own achievements, one has to internalize, for instance, the values and behavior patterns of the status group which one aspires to enter. However, Dreitzel explicitly rejects any overestimation of the success criterion set out in Pareto's writings. In industrial society success is always based, among other things, on performance, and purely "Machiavellian" success elites are therefore the exception (ibid.: 103). His second proviso is rooted in the fact that many top positions are in fact hereditary, as in the case of single owners of large family businesses, members of the higher nobility, or the last remaining big landowners. These top positions, are, in Dreitzel's view, thus not actually elite positions but a "relict from bourgeois-capitalist or even corporatist-feudalist social orders" (ibid.: 143). He concludes that the upper strata of democratic industrial society is accordingly made up of two components: one with inherited positions of power and prestige, the other consisting of those who have earned their positions by dint of their achievements and professional careers. The latter group is dominant in society and its elites, whereas the former is clearly diminishing in importance.

3.3 "Strategic Elites" (Suzanne Keller)

The most comprehensive attempt made thus far to clarify analytically the position and function of elites was undertaken in 1963 by Suzanne Keller[21] in her book *Beyond the Ruling Class*. According to Keller's initial definition, elites are effective and responsible minorities that are entrusted with the task of realizing society's principle goals and securing the continuity of the social order, and that are efficient in the pursuit of these goals. Elites in this sense are, she argues, one of the primary forces supporting any organized society. The growing internal differentiation of modern industrial society leads to an appreciable increase in both the number and the significance of elites, which can no longer be adequately described using outmoded concepts like ruling class, caste, or aristocracy (Keller 1963: 4–5).[22]

As the subtitle of her book – *Strategic Elites in Modern Society* – indicates, Keller introduces the term strategic elites as a central concept of her analysis. She sees a fundamental difference between those, such as beauty queens or bridge champions, who are only of significance in their own field, and those who are of significance for society as a whole because their decisions and actions have consequences for many members of society. It is the latter in whom Keller is interested and whom she terms "strategic elites" (ibid.: 20).

Keller sees strategic elites on the whole as being the result of four social forces effective in society: increase in its size, its internal division of labor, its formal organization, and its moral diversity. These forces ensure that individual functional elites – e.g. the political, economic, academic, religious, cultural elites – become increasingly autonomous in organizational, professional, and moral terms. In modern industrial society this differentiation has advanced so far that the central tasks of elites – symbolizing moral unity, coordinating various activities, resolving conflicts, and providing protection from external enemies – can no longer be realized by a single uniform elite. A single hierarchical pyramid with an elite at its top is replaced by a multitude of parallel pyramids, and hence of elites. It is therefore no longer correct to assume the existence of an all-powerful "economic ruling class." Economic power still exists but, even in a society that worships the market, it is only one of several equally important forces. For instance, the business elite, better organized today than in the past, has less influence than it once had (ibid.: 82–3). For Keller the transition from the "ruling class" of the past to the "strategic elites" of modern industrial society both involves coexistence of a number of elites instead of a single elite and has key consequences for the central characteristics of elites. Hence strategic elites are always, by reason of their functional specialization, smaller, more short-lived, of more limited authority, and above all more open than ruling classes, because access to them is based on specialized knowledge and individual effort rather than on birth and wealth (ibid.: 57–8).

In providing a systematic description of the social function of strategic elites Keller falls back on Talcott Parsons' theoretical framework. Using his well-known AGIL paradigm (adaptation, goal attainment, integration, latent pattern maintenance),[23] she distinguishes four basic types of strategic elite which she sees as providing the necessary link between the abstract model of society and its actual reality. The political elite is primarily responsible for the decision as to which goals are to be pursued, and by what means, when, and where they are to be pursued; the economic, academic, military, and diplomatic elites are responsible for providing the necessary means; the integrative elite, consisting of outstanding representatives of church, philosophy, education, and the "first families," assume the task of formulating moral standards and convictions; and the elites consisting of artists, writers, entertainers, film stars, and athletes provide for the maintenance of the individual citizen's everyday morals. Keller calls those responsible for the first two groups of tasks external elites, referring to the other two groups as internal elites.

The external elites are considerably better organized than the internal elites, since they are far more dependent for their success on the direct cooperation of a large number of other people. A top manager cannot do his work without the other employees in his company, whereas a writer or painter is entirely free to work alone at home. The more bureaucratic a sector is, the more organized are its elites. There is one more important difference between these two types of elite. The criterion by which their performance is measured is, in the case of the first type, their efficiency, while in the second case it is the impression they make in public. Political, economic, academic, military, and diplomatic elites are judged, Keller argues, by the tangible results of their work, such as improvement of standards of living or military victories, while religious, cultural, or entertainment elites are judged on the basis of their intangible success in questions bearing on general mood, satisfaction, will to live, or fear of death (ibid.: 96–8).

In view of the fact that there is no universally valid hierarchy of values, the social position of the various elites in a society depends, in Keller's view, on specific historical givens. In her view, military and religious elites hold the highest positions in societies marked by universal material want, while these positions are in the hands of political and economic elites – and will, in the future, presumably be held by scientific and cultural elites as well – in societies in possession of the resources needed to abolish want. Modern industrial societies are in this respect on the path from the second to the third stage. Due to their functional differentiation, there is no longer any durable hierarchy among their elites, though the existence of short-term, limited hierarchies is certainly conceivable, indeed even likely (ibid.: 124–7).

In Keller's view, the existence of various strategic elites poses another major problem in addition to that of functional coordination. The more complex and differentiated the structure of elites and, accordingly, the greater the relative autonomy of individual elites, the more difficult it is to develop or preserve a uniform canon of values. In the end, every elite has to represent both its own specific sector and the general value system held by society as a whole. However, common goals and values are crucial to all elites if, in view of a situation marked by mutual interdependencies, there is to be any guarantee that society as a whole is to function. These shared goals and values also facilitate communication between individual elites as well as personal contact among their members. This in turn fosters the development and stabilization of a value consensus, which is as a rule all the more effective the more covertly it operates. Mutual conflicts can only be resolved productively on a solid foundation of this kind (ibid.: 145–9).

Although it is crucially important that such a consensus be developed, there is, in Keller's view, one further obstacle in its way: altered recruitment patterns for elite positions, which undermine social homogeneity, once a factor that fostered a common canon of values. Of the two basic principles of the selection of elites, birth on the one hand and performance and merit on the other, the latter is coming more and more to prevail in modern industrial society. Societies subject to continuous growth and differentiation simply need elites with specialized training and modern knowledge. Skills and knowledge passed down through the family are no longer sufficient (ibid.: 190). The recruitment base is accordingly becoming broader in social terms. Elite positions can no longer be filled by members of a single class; indeed, depending on the function in question, candidates for such positions must be recruited from the various strata and classes of society.

Keller uses the US to supply concrete examples for her arguments. She assumes here that the role played by social origin in the recruitment of elites decreases in significance as achievement grows in importance as a selection criterion (ibid.: 205). In her opinion, the empirical data back this assumption. The majority of elites stem from the middle classes, in particular from families of medium-level, businesspeople, and professionals. The substantial differences in income, status, and training typical of the middle classes are therefore a shaping factor in the make-up of elites. While, as she notes, the working class is – with the possible exception of entertainment, education, religion, and sports – as yet markedly underrepresented, the share it accounts for in sectors previously as good as inaccessible to it – e.g. in business – is on the increase (ibid.: 206–7). Keller concedes, however, that the proportion of members of the elite from the upper and upper middle classes increases as a function of the level of the positions in question, noting that if the concept of elite is regarded in a very narrow sense, the influence of class origin and status remains very strong, though no longer all-powerful. Furthermore, she sees a marked trend toward social opening (ibid.: 210), with the circulation of members of the elite today proceeding at a faster pace than ever before (ibid.: 251).

While social origin, Keller notes by way of summary, is still of importance, and privileged groups still tend to constitute the majority in some elites, wealth and high social status – which may be still advantageous in some elites – are no longer the decisive factors involved in gaining access to top positions in business, politics, and culture. And while it is true that the connection between material resources and educational opportunities is still the source of an unequal distribution of chances of success, first, elite members of privileged family origin are able to gain and hold their positions only through hard work, achievement, and effort, and second, elites are in the end forced to open up to candidates of "lower class and lower status." This serves to weaken and possibly even break the age-old connection between elite status and upper-class status (ibid.: 216–17).

All in all, Keller notes in her final chapter, individual achievement has replaced social origin as the "chief principle of recruitment to strategic elites" in modern industrial society. This, however, implies that membership in the higher echelons of the social hierarchy, which without doubt continues to exist, can no longer be passed on by virtue of birth from one generation to the next; instead, the conditions for access are redefined in each new generation. After all, Keller remarks, the crucial qualifications for access to elites cannot be handed down but must be acquired through individual attainment. This, she asserts, makes it impossible for a ruling class to emerge (ibid.: 262–9).

At the end of the book Keller deals with what she considers to be the most important problems and dangers for the future: equality, freedom, and despotism. Her prognosis is a positive one. As far as equality is concerned, she writes, disparities in income, status, power, etc., are not eliminated by the shift from ruling classes, aristocracies, or castes to strategic elites, but an increase in number of such elites clearly goes hand in hand with an enlargement of equality of opportunity. In the case of freedom and despotism,

Keller writes, certain important risks, including the dangers posed by expertocracy, psychological habituation to power, and a growing distance between elites and the general population, should not be underestimated. These dangers are, however, substantially limited by the heterogeneity of strategic elites, since the various elites exercise a measure of control on one another, and limited power generally means less abuse of power. Furthermore, public discussion on elites and social problems, together with the population's improving standard of education, also serve to limit these risks. At best, elites constitute temporary aristocracies over which the general public, in their various roles as electorate, audience, or consumers, are now in a better position than ever before to exercise control. The age-old dream of a society ruled by achievement and not by force is, in Keller's view, thus gradually becoming reality. Even so, Keller notes, the danger of "tyranny" has not yet been banished for ever, though at present the danger is not a tyranny of the "haves" over the "have-nots" but of experts over laypersons. Keller's final conclusion is that the best approach is simply to assume that all members of society, and above all members of elites, are in possession of an adequate understanding of our complex social order (ibid.: 269–79).

3.4 Functional elites and consensus

Research on elites has never again regained the theoretical level it had attained during the first two post-war decades. At present the picture is dominated by (more or less broad) empirical studies, most of which refer back – and usually in very brief form – to theoretical approaches devoted to pluralist functional elites. Thematically, these studies are concerned primarily with the problem of whether or, as the case may be, how it may be possible to achieve the consensus necessary for the functioning of a democratic parliamentary system. One typical example of this approach is a recent comprehensive survey on elites conducted at the German University of Potsdam (Bürklin and Rebenstorf 1997). Of its roughly 500 pages, only five are concerned with fundamental theoretical considerations, and only half of these are devoted to an overview of the present state of research on elites, the other half dealing with the main thematic focus of the survey itself: "Consensus and conflict as a framework condition for the behavior and activities of elites" (ibid.: 18–21).[24] This study thus continues unreflectedly on in the footsteps of the Mannheim studies on elites, which were likewise characterized by a general lack of concern with theoretical considerations and a concentration on the question of consensus among elites (Hoffmann-Lange *et al.* 1980; Wildenmann *et al.* 1982).[25]

In her 1981 analysis of the Mannheim elite project Hoffmann-Lange sums up her central findings on these studies devoted to the issue of cooperation and conflict among elites as follows.[26] West German elites, she contends, show marked differences in attitude "along the two conflict lines constitutive of the German party system": those concerned with economic, sociopolitical issues and those having to do with social questions (sociomoral problems and individual liberties). However, only the first of these complexes – where the lies of conflict run parallel to the sectoral boundaries between business and labor union elites – is structurally anchored in elites. As far as the second complex is concerned, however, membership in a given sectoral elite is no longer a relevant factor. Here attitudes are said to be bound up "primarily with the values held by individuals." But irrespective of these controversies, it is asserted, there is a general consensus among all elites as regards the rules to be observed in playing out conflicts. Heterogeneous social origins and differences in – primarily sectoral – career trajectories mean that while there is relatively little "social cohesion" among elites, and the structural conditions required for an integration of elites are generally not given, the elite network is, for all practical purposes, no less dense in Germany than it is in other countries. Almost all elites are represented in the core of this network, and it also includes persons active in more than one policy field. In this way the network contributes equally to integrating sectors and interlinking various policy fields. Contrary to Dahrendorf's opinion, an integration of elites is, in her words, also possible "among socially heterogeneous and professionally specialized elites." The central sector here is said to be the political, a fact which ensures it a large measure of autonomy (Hoffmann-Lange 1992: 402–7).

Although they, too, assume the existence of functional elites, G. Lowell Field and John Higley have developed, since the end of the 1970s, a theoretical (and now very influential) approach which calls for a more marked return to the classic elite theories of Michels, Mosca, and Pareto and their productive link with the functionalist model. Field and Higley, whose political critique focuses on the welfare state and its ideology, concur with the classic theorists in asserting that elites are inevitable in societies of any complexity, although they also deem it necessary to reject the notion of a universal and objective validity of values like "equality, liberty and freedom" (Field and Higley 1980: 3, 72). Elites, they argue, are not only the inevitable product of any form of bureaucratic structure, the persons with strategic positions in these bureaucracies – i.e. elites – inevitably show a tendency to assert their positions and to pass some of their advantages on to relatives, friends, and associates (ibid.: 71). In this context Field and Higley go so far as to speak of a considerable degree of inheritability. In their opinion this is necessary, it being the only inducement for elites to keep up their interest in their positions and to ensure that they continue to function smoothly. It is for this reason that it is difficult to forge links between the normative notions of freedom and equality.

For Field and Higley, elite formation is thus fundamentally and factually heavily dependent on levels of socioeconomic development, and both elites and the attitudes of nonelites can be assigned to four different stages of development (ibid.: 18–21). They point out, for instance, that a largely uniform ruling class and a good measure of egalitarianism on the part of nonelites were typical of the underdeveloped agrarian societies characteristic of Europe up to the sixteenth century and for the rest of the world up to the twentieth century. By contrast, industrialized societies are typified equally by an egalitarian or managerial orientation, i.e. one that accepts hierarchies, and three types of elite: the consensus elite (as in the UK or the US), the incompletely unified elite (as in the Federal Republic of Germany, Italy, and Japan in the 1950s), and the ideologically unified elite (as in fascism). Today's Western industrial societies are characterized by nonelites with a managerial orientation and a uniform elite geared to consensus. Their uniformity is said to consist basically in a lack of members of elites who organize and formulate hostile-oppositional nonelite orientations (ibid.: 37–8). The established forms in which conflicts are played out are accepted by all elites, a fact that serves to defuse conflicts and thus to stabilize the political order.

According to the core proposition of Field and Higley's (self-styled) "elitist" model, the main actors involved in any process of fundamental change are always the elites themselves. Nonelites "can usually do little or nothing to promote the consensual unification of a disunified elite" (ibid.: 77). Furthermore, nonelites are rarely in agreement on, or indeed even interested in, important political issues. Political stability is, they note, for this reason never the result of voluntary, peaceable, and sufficiently informed cooperation among all social actors. Instead, they go on, political stability is invariably the artificial product of a continuous series of prudent decisions taken by the influential and politically active, that is to say, by elites (ibid.: 117–18). The existence of consensus elites which act in this manner is an indispensable prerequisite for today's Western democracy. This model, it is argued, is also bound to certain socioeconomic conditions which have developed only under rare and more or less chance circumstances in industrialized Western countries, a fact which makes it impossible to export it to other regions of the world. Should this civilization ever be abandoned, it will therefore never again exist in this or any similar fashion (ibid.: 116). Field and Higley conclude by stating that it is essential to combat the ideology of the welfare state and to avert any escalation of future threats of confrontation by ensuring that elites are given the frame of reference which they urgently need for self-assured political action (ibid.: 130).

3.5 Summary

The two basic premises shared by all functionalist approaches to elites are:

1   In modern societies there is no longer a uniform ruling class or elite; here we find only individual, functional subelites that compete with one another at the top levels of the key sectors of society. Nor is there any sign of an unambiguous domination by the economic elite of other subelites in politics, science, culture, etc.

2   In principle these elites are accessible to everyone, since elite positions are filled primarily on the basis of (sector-specific) performance criteria. Performance has thus replaced inheritance as the key principle in elite recruitment. As a result, elites, far from being homogeneous, have now become socially heterogeneous. The observable preponderance in elites of the upper strata of society is due above all to their better access to institutions of higher learning.

For the large majority of pluralist elite researchers these premises pose a central question: how is it possible, under the conditions implied by the existence of rival and socially heterogeneous subelites, to secure the cooperation among elites that is necessary if society is to function? What is to provide for the necessary cohesion and value consensus among the various elites if there is no longer any common basis rooted in membership in the upper class?

At first sight the answers to this question may appear to diverge widely. While, for example, Dahrendorf's early writings saw the solution to the problem in an established elite on the British model, including elite educational institutions and career paths, it is precisely this type of consensus elite that Field and Higley criticize, rejecting it unambiguously as obsolete and, in the long run, even dangerous. However, despite all their differences, a closer look shows that there is a kind of red thread running through them, which almost all the social scientists involved in the debate follow either explicitly or implicitly in their argumentation. This is their conviction that elites, if they are to reach a consensus among themselves, can at best pay only little heed to the public at large (and its interests and views). Dreitzel sums up the matter in a brief, succinct sentence when he says, "The term elite designates the ideal type of leading groups in our society in that it points to the principle of meritocracy under which these groups lead and the mass follows" (Dreitzel 1962: 154).

This position is, understandably, formulated most clearly by those authors who are less critical of the classic elite sociology of Michels, Mosca, and Pareto and build directly on their work. Of the older authors, these would mainly include Lasswell, Kaplan, and Kornhauser, and the younger group would include Field and Higley. They view elites as the central or even sole guarantors of the stability of Western democracies and consequently see in any major influence by the masses on important political decisions a substantial threat to these democracies. This influence, they argue, must be reduced as far as possible, while the scopes open to elites must be enlarged to permit elites to reach consensus among themselves and then translate this consensus into political practice.

Although most representatives of the theory of functional elites do not share this pronounced stance, they do concur (be it consciously or unconsciously) with some of the central points of the argument. For instance, Dahrendorf's long-standing preference for the British model is reminiscent of the ideas put forward by Lasswell and Kaplan or Field and Higley, inasmuch as they see consensus among established elites as the surest safeguard of democratically constituted societies; Keller, too, sees one of the greatest threats to democracy in exaggerated demands for democracy, equality, and public accountability of leaders, and she calls on elites not to deny or seek to veil their elite status as such and instead to openly and assertively accept it (Keller 1963: 192, 220). In her concluding remarks concerning the risk that these very elites may prove arrogant and insensitive "to the problems of human life," Keller can, in essence, only appeal to the humanity and understanding of elites. The principle task of modern society, creation of better living conditions, "depends on the skills and the vision – and humanity – of the strategic elites" (ibid.: 279). How closely related these positions of "elitists" like Field and Higley and representatives of the pluralist theory of functional elites – two schools that appear at first sight to be totally at odds with one another – in fact are, is underlined not least by the fact that Hoffmann-Lange, a prominent representative of the second school, published a study together with Higley (and Kadushin and Moore) which is quite clearly shaped by the argumentation and conclusions of Field and Higley (Higley *et al.* 1991).

The principle reason behind this congruence of views is, above all, one central weakness in the functionalist theoretical approach to elites. While most functionalist studies do go into the relationship between elites and classes, they fail to deepen the matter thoroughly enough to adequately explain the power differentials between the elites in various sectors of society: the manner in which they are grounded in the social structure or the role played in this process by the various classes and strata of the population as a whole. As long as this approach, as is usually the case, focuses only on formal and – in this case – tangible political power structures, the inevitable effect is that a good share of the real power relations at work in society is disregarded.

This critique applies as well for the network analyses commonly used today in attempts to measure the density of contacts both within and between individual elites. These analyses generally get no further than the surface because they focus primarily on formal contacts. What this implies is that the functionalist approach as a whole is relatively static in nature. It is not able to adequately identify changes in the play of forces in society as a whole – including those at work among elites – that have made themselves felt since the 1980s in most industrialized Western nations under the flag of neoliberalism.[27] For all these reasons this approach– and this is the reason for its predilection for the classic dichotomy of elite and mass – tends in the end to be a rather unhistorical and abstract approach the key criterion of which is the stability of existing parliamentary systems rather than the actual situation of the population at large.

Questions

1   How does Mannheim distinguish between the diverse types of elites?
2   How do the German and US elite theories of the fifties and sixties describe the relationship between elites and democracy?
3   What does Keller understand by the "strategic elites"?
4   How do you define the term "functional elites"?
5   How do the functional elite theories explain the process of achieving a consensus among the competing subelites?

4   Elites and classes

The central reference point for all analyses which, whether explicitly or more implicitly, deal critically with the functionalist approach is the relationship between elites and classes. This applies for the two most prominent representatives of critical elite research, Mills with his "Power Elite" (Mills 1956 [1959]) and Bourdieu with his "Classe dominante" (Bourdieu 1979 [1984], 1989a [1996], 1993b), but also to authors such as Domhoff (1967, 1971, 1978, 1980, 1983) and Dye (1976, 1979, 1983, 1985, 1990, 1995), whose numerous studies on elites in the US are oriented to either Mills' "Power Elite" or Marx's concept of the ruling class, or authors like de Saint Martin (1993), who worked for many years with Bourdieu, and her study on the French aristocracy. They all seek to explain elites with reference to their position vis-à-vis the other classes and strata of society. They challenge "pluralist" elite theories wherever these show critical weaknesses.

4.1 *The Power Elite* (C. Wright Mills)

In *The Power Elite*[1], probably the best-known of his books, C. Wright Mills[2] early on gives the following general definition of elite: the "the power elite is composed of men whose positions enable them ... to make decisions having major consequences" (Mills 1959: 4). In Mills' view the men of the elite are those at the head of the large economic, political, and military organizations, which he sees as the only organizations able to confer on them their great and, above all, durable power. These three sectors form the "real centers of power," and other sectors such as churches, universities, or the family are subordinate to them in that it is the former rather than the latter that determine the major developments in society. Decisions made in their highly centralized power apparatuses are increasingly interdependent and their structures are growingly interwoven, and intensive coordination is therefore unavoidable. In the end, the overlaps between the domains of power and the interdependence between them induce the powerful leaders of these three groups to "come together to form the power elite of America" (ibid.: 9).

However, the power elite owes its rise and its stability not only to the intertwinement of the three sectors and the identity of their interests but also rests, as Mills succinctly puts it, "upon the similarity of origin and outlook and the social and political intermingling of the top circles from each of these dominant hierarchies" (ibid.: 292). Although there is no aristocracy whose leading families decide on the distribution of top positions, most of the members of the power elite do come from the upper strata, that is, at least from families of academics or businesspeople. They have generally attended a university, frequently the famed private elite universities, their educational careers are similar in nature, and they are often marked by similar features such as religion or place of birth. Social origin alone, however, does not, for Mills, permit any final conclusions to be drawn with regard to the psychological and social ties that link the members of the power elite. It is also necessary to take a look at the recruitment and value standards valid within the various circles belonging to the power elite, since these provide – possibly even more than anything else – for the power elite's homogeneity. With the requirements placed on the leading men from the three sectors becoming increasingly similar, the training and selection of these men themselves finally serve to make them increasingly alike. Their manifold professional and personal contacts cement their common features even further, and it therefore can be said that nowhere in America is "there as great a 'class consciousness' as among the elite" (ibid.: 283).

These general remarks on the power elite are based on detailed analyses of all the important actors, the results of which Mills presents in the nine previous chapters of his book. He devotes approximately two-thirds of his comments to the propertied class that is, the upper class in the country and in the leading metropolitan regions, the wealthy, the "chief executives" and the "corporate rich." It is these people in whom he is primarily interested.

Mills characterizes the upper class, that is, the "first families" in town and country as "a propertied class" which is distinguished from other sections of the population by its similar lifestyle, similar educational and professional careers, intensive contacts within the group, and a marked awareness of its own special position. These people live in the same exclusive areas, wear the same type of dress, attend clubs accessible only to their own circles, and generally tend to have close contacts with each other. Since many members are in positions of power, the close personal contacts and mutual trust and confidence naturally mean that problems are discussed in informal conversations. In this way their children effortlessly learn how important decisions are made. This in turn tends to blur the boundaries between personal matters and matters of interest to society as a whole. Social "'background' is one way in which, on the basis of intimate association, the activities of an upper class may be tacitly co-ordinated" (ibid.: 69). This is true at the local no less than at the national level. The tone is set by the upper echelons in the metropolises, and it is they who are at the top of the power and status hierarchy of the country as a whole.[3]

The conflict between "old and new wealth," ubiquitous and constant, is always resolved by the acceptance of the nouveau riche into the circle of the upper classes, though this may not always occur immediately, indeed some-times not until the second generation. The renowned schools and universi-ties in which the offspring of these circles are educated play, in Mills' view, an extremely important role here. At these institutions they learn to adopt common behavioral patterns, norms, and values, thus ensuring, more than any other institutions, the uniformity of the upper class and a blending of the "old" and "new" families. For Mills this is the "one clue to the national unity of the upper social classes in America today" (ibid.: 64). All in all, the American upper class is, thanks to specifically American historical con-ditions (no aristocracy), "merely an enriched bourgeoisie;" access to this class is ultimately determined by money and not by the family tree (ibid.: 50).

Mills argues that it is the owners of "large fortunes," the multimillion-aires, who are at the top of this upper class; about three quarters of them come from rich families, and the fathers of roughly the same percentage of them are or were entrepreneurs. Wealth, then, is not only inherited but also shows a tendency "to monopolize new opportunities for getting 'great wealth'" (ibid.: 105). Even so, unlike the past, multimillionaires no longer "reign alone on top of visible and simple hierarchies" but are increasingly bound up in the power hierarchies of large corporations, for today it is the large corporations, and not large fortunes, that are the source and basis of lasting wealth and power. In these organized centers of the owning class, then, rich families ally themselves with top executives, the administrators of their assets, either by combining the functions involved, through coopera-tion, or on the basis of common interests (ibid.: 117). The men at the top of the large corporations who do not themselves come from the rich families at least have a similar social background, more than 70 percent of their fathers being entrepreneurs or academics, and only 10 percent of them workers or white-collar workers – in many cases already the second generation and in situations that remain relatively constant for decades (ibid.: 128).

All these people profit from the prestige associated with leading positions in national corporations, since "members of society," both big-city and local, draw their standards of prestige from precisely these corporations (ibid.: 85). The big-city upper class, "the upper 400," not having managed to become the "center of a national system of prestige," and celebrities from sports and entertainment being "ephemeral figures" without power of any stable sort, and since the elite is in need of "some sort of organization of enduring and stable prestige," much is to be said in favor of the business elite joining together with the political and military elites to form one single prestige system, sidelining show-business and sports stars (ibid.: 90–1).

For Mills, the rise of the large corporations has, generally speaking, not only led to a concentration of power but also to greater inner cohesion among the owning class. Since most shares are held by multimillionaires and the chief executives of the major corporations, and in view of the reciprocal connections implied by posts on executive and supervisory boards, these persons have expanded their vision beyond the individual corporation to embrace the interests of large-scale industry as a whole and, ultimately, the interests of their entire class. Their decisions determine the course of the economy, employment rates, purchasing power, prices, and investment levels. It is not the "visible" politicians but "the chief executives who sit in the political directorate" who thus "hold the power and the means of defending the privileges of their corporate world." No power effectively can resist them (ibid.: 125).[4]

At a later point Mills qualifies the impression he may have made with formulations of this kind. The political apparatus, he says, is not merely an "extension of the corporate world," the American government not "in any simple way . . . a committee of 'the ruling class.'" It is instead "a network of committees" whose members are also recruited from representatives of the political and military hierarchies (ibid.: 170). Here Mills lodges a protest against any interpretation which would attribute political rule to the propertied class, and in particular against "the simple Marxian view" that sees in the "big economic man the real holder of power" (ibid.: 277), and seeks to explain social developments simply as a reflection of the "will of the bourgeoisie" (ibid.: 16). In a long footnote he makes his point even more clearly. It is here that he explains his reasons for using the term "power elite" instead of "ruling class." In his opinion the term "ruling class" is too fraught with connotations. Class is an economic term, rule a political concept. Thus the term "ruling class" implies a theory according to which an economic class exercises political rule. This simplified theory may or may not hold true for limited periods of time, but, Mills notes, he has no desire to drag this term into the concepts he employs, preferring instead to use more precise and generally valid concepts. Above all, he states, his aim is to counter the risk involved in the general usage of the term "ruling class," that is, the risk that the autonomy of the political elite might otherwise be underestimated. The representatives of all three sectors, business, politics, and the military, frequently have a considerable degree of autonomy in today's world and are obliged to make and enforce their most important decisions by seeking to forge alliances (ibid.: 250).

However, Mills adds, the political elite has lost much of its influence in recent years, whereas the military elite has gained in influence, so that "the corporate rich and the high warlord, in their coinciding interests, rule." This mirrors the increased importance of both foreign and security policy and the fact that the economy "is at once a permanent-war economy and a private-corporation economy" (ibid.: 275–7). The US military, which, because of the country's geographical situation and its traditional citizen-soldier system, was long without any particularly large role in society, has grown very substantially in importance as a result of the world-political situation and the destruction potential of today's weapons (ibid.: 175–6). Not only does the military have increasingly close connections with industry, it has also become the largest sponsor and planner of research and science, in this way extending its influence into the education sector as well (ibid.: 216–18).

The development of the political elite has gone the opposite way. It is above all two trends (in addition to the changes in foreign policy) that are seen here as responsible for its perceptible decline in importance. First, the replacement of the old, fading middle class consisting of farmers and self-employed persons by the new class of white-collar employees. These, however, lack the economic autonomy of the old middle class and are thus "powerless," whereas the old class held, for a time, an "independent base of power," grounded in personally owned property. Second, the organized working class, which appeared on the stage as a new political force in the 1930s, did not, contrary to initial impressions, develop into a "power-bloc independent of corporation and state." In fact, Mills goes on, this class soon lost some of its clout as a result of its increasing dependence on the machinery of government, and today it is involved only in small ways in the making of important decisions. Its leaders no longer have access to the national elite and are forced to be content with their role at the middle level of power (ibid.: 262–3).

The struggle for power between large and small-scale property owners and the new force of the workers, who under the New Deal policies of the 1930s had provided the political elite with unusually large scopes of action, is now, in Mills' opinion, a thing of the past. Another thing of the past is the relative balance of forces, which the dominant power of the industrial bloc, unable to eliminate it wholly, had at least managed to challenge and contain. This also spelled the end of the foundation on which the powerful position of politics was built. At that time, Mills explains, real politicians stood at the head of the state, but these have now been replaced by "political men, and not by economic and military men turned political" (ibid.: 273). Today these persons are dominant in the upper ranks of politics, while professional politicians have lost considerable ground to them. For Mills, government now consists principally of outsiders, mainly men from the business world who have as a rule achieved office by way of cooptation rather than having to work their way up the ladder as professional politicians. One inevitable concomitant of this process is that it has served to strengthen the executive branch at the expense of the legislative (ibid.: 229–30). The idea that there is such a thing as a balance of forces is thus out of step with reality. Today, Mills argues, there is such a balance only at the middle level of power in municipalities and in individual regions, and then only when the concern is local issues which do not collide with the interests of the truly powerful (ibid.: 268).

All in all, Mills sums up, American society breaks down into three distinct segments. At the top, a genuine "elite of power" has developed, the middle levels consist of "a drifting set of stalemated, balancing forces" no longer able to forge links between the lower and the upper levels, and the lower level is politically fragmented and "growing increasingly powerless." It is at this level that a mass society has developed (ibid.: 368). Mass society differs in four respects from classic public society. Instead of being actively formulated and discussed by individual citizens, opinions are passively absorbed from the mass media; there is virtually no room for deviant positions; the state controls the ways in which opinion is translated into action; and the mass now "has no autonomy from institutions" (ibid.: 304). The reason why all this is possible is that people in mass society (above all in big cities) live in isolation from one another "sunk in their routines," uninterested in participating in public life (ibid.: 320). Instead of viewing them in social contexts, they see their personal troubles and worries as disjointed, individual questions. There is a lack of political education and discussion. This all makes it possible to manipulate the mass. Thus "the idea of a mass society suggests the idea of an elite of power" (ibid.: 323). The autonomous associations which in the past "[stood] between the various classes and the state" are losing their political effectiveness and being replaced by centralized organizations which, using all the means of power at their disposal, are taking "charge of the terrorized or – as the case may be – merely intimidated society of masses" (ibid.: 310).

4.2 The reproduction of the ruling class (Pierre Bourdieu)

The analysis of the social elite or the "dominant or ruling class" likewise plays a central role in Pierre Bourdieu's[5] theory. Unlike Mills, however, Bourdieu is concerned less with the way in which the political system functions than with the mechanisms that reproduce the "dominant class." When asked by Loïc J.D. Wacquant in an interview conducted on the occasion of the publication of "La Noblesse d'Etat" about the reasons for the book, Bourdieu replied that he believed that "in advanced societies" it was not possible to investigate "the 'ruling class,' the 'elite,' the 'dominant class' . . . without elucidating the conditions under which they reproduce themselves" (Bourdieu 1993b: 19).

He first addressed the issue in his early studies on the French education system (Bourdieu and Passeron 1964 [1979]).[6] Bourdieu further developed his theory in studies on the general significance of academic titles for the reproduction of classes, and in particular of the ruling class (Bourdieu 1974; Bourdieu and Boltanski 1975; Bourdieu et al. 1973 [1977]) as well as on the role of class-specific habitus in this process (Bourdieu 1979 [1984]), later deepening and rounding off his theory in studies on individual segments of the ruling class (Bourdieu 1984 [1988], Bourdieu and de Saint Martin 1978, 1982) and, finally, on the "field of power"[7] as a whole (Bourdieu 1989a [1996]; Bourdieu and de Saint Martin 1987).

Two propositions form the point of departure of Bourdieu's reflections:

1   Academic careers are largely dependent on the social background of school and university students.
2   The process of structural economic change forces the dominant faction

of the ruling class – whose power extends to the business world – to radically alter its reproduction strategies, a shift that greatly increases the weight accorded to academic degrees in filling top positions.

With regard to the first point, Bourdieu sees discrepancies in academic success – which tend to differ as a function of parental background – as due primarily to the unequal endowment of families with economic and cultural capital. The acquisition of academic titles as an institutionalized and thus socially accepted form of cultural capital is dependent on the cultural capital of which a family is already in possession. Since cultural capital can only be accumulated personally, through "internalization," and is thus "fundamentally embodied" and lays claim to considerable personal time, primary socialization in the family appears to be either "a positive value (a gain in time, a head start) or a negative value (wasted time, and doubly so because more time must be spent correcting its effects)" (Bourdieu 1983 [1997]: 48). Cultural capital can be accumulated from earliest childhood on, without any loss of time or substance, only where the entire time invested in family upbringing is at the same time a period of accumulation (ibid.: 49). Furthermore, availability of economic capital is not the only thing required for this internal family teaching/learning process – families, and as a rule mothers, have to be able to afford the time they need for the purpose – economic capital also improves the chances of such children to acquire a higher academic qualification by making it possible for them to postpone their entry into working life in favor of a protracted phase of education and training (ibid.: 54). The more cultural and economic capital available to a family, the earlier the acquisition process can begin, the more effective it will later prove in school and university, and the longer it can be protracted (ibid.: 49–50).

As regards the second point, Bourdieu sees the central impact of the process of structural change in the economy as a whole as well as in individual companies in the fact that traditional family businesses are increasingly being superseded by large corporations as well as in the growing differentiation, complexity, and bureaucratization of internal and external business relationships. Career trajectories within companies are generally depersonalized and rationalized, with the result that official academic titles have become far more important than ever before. A diploma from a "Grande école" "tends to become a necessary (but not sufficient) condition of access to positions of economic power" – and the larger the corporation, the more this applies (Bourdieu *et al.* 1973 [1977]: 200).[8] The dominant faction of the ruling class, whose power rests principally on the possession of economic capital, is forced to adapt its reproduction strategies to altered conditions. Whereas in the past executive positions inherited as family-owned companies were passed on to the next generation, today the focus is on acquiring exclusive academic titles. Part of the existing economic capital is transformed into institutionalized cultural capital with a view to securing the claims of offspring to top positions and power in corporations (ibid.:

209). Even so, economic capital also retains its direct power beyond this process of transformation. It is, for example, far easier for the offspring of entrepreneurs to do without prestigious academic degrees (particularly those of the Grandes écoles) than it is for their rivals (ibid.: 221–2), and the incomes they earn with the same qualifications, Bourdieu continues, are also considerably higher, because all this amounts to a "dissimulated form of appropriation of profit" (ibid.: 209, 225).[9]

In his later writings Bourdieu deepens his analysis of reproduction mechanisms in two distinct directions. First, he deals in greater detail with the role of the Grandes écoles in this process (Bourdieu 1989a [1996], 1993; Bourdieu and de Saint Martin 1987); and second, he looks more closely into the significance of habitus[10] for these reproduction strategies (Bourdieu 1979 [1984], 1992, 1993a; Bourdieu and Wacquant 1992). For Bourdieu, habitus is a key factor in this context in that it represents the internalization of "a determinate type of social and economic condition" (Bourdieu and Wacquant 1992: 105) and it thus determines (as a rule unconsciously) the strategies that are pursued, or indeed can, generally, be pursued.[11]

Bourdieu sees a person's habitus as mediating between this person's position in social space and his or her lifestyle. Habitus is a system of dispositions, a general, basic stance which determines a person's perception, feeling, thinking, behavior, and which, more than anything else, marks the boundaries drawn for every individual by his social origin and position. In an interview Bourdieu outlines these boundaries as follows: "A person who has, for example, a petty-bourgeois habitus, simply has, as Marx says, boundaries in his brain which he cannot cross. He for this reason finds certain things simply unthinkable, impossible" (Bourdieu 1992: 33).

Anyone who has grown up in a working-class family, Bourdieu notes, will dress differently from someone whose father was a senior physician, he or she will like different food, enjoy different films and music, will be fond of different sports and leisure activities, have different reading and learning habits, speak a different language, have other career plans and a different circle of friends. The experiences, individual and collective, of the individual and his family and class will have become embodied in his habitus. While it is of course impossible that all members of a class should have precisely the same experiences in exactly the same order, the chances of their being confronted with situations typical for their class are far greater than they are for members of other classes (Bourdieu 1980 [1990]: 59–60). This is the basis of the class-specific habitus, which thus represents "embodied class" (Bourdieu 1979 [2004]: 437).

Bourdieu draws his distinctions on grounds of the volume of capital available to three major classes: the dominant class, the petty-bourgeoisie, or lower middle classes, and the "classe populaire," or lower classes. These can then be further broken down into various factions, depending on the actual distribution of the economic and cultural capital they possess. Each of these classes has its own characteristic habitus: the ruling class the habitus of distinction and legitimate taste, the petty-bourgeoisie a habitus driven by striving and educational ambition, and the "popular class" the habitus of necessity and popular taste. Bourdieu focuses in particular on the difference between the habituses of the ruling class and the petty-bourgeoisie, because he sees habitus as defining the boundaries of the field of power and the limits set to the social aspirations of members of the petty-bourgeoisie. For Bourdieu, the central element of the habitus of the dominant class is its self-assurance, which is felt by its members to be "necessary, that is, as a materi-alized coincidence of 'is' and 'ought.'" It "supports and authorizes all the inner or manifest forms of *certitudo sui*, casualness, grace, facility, elegance, freedom, in a word naturalness" opposed to the "petit-bourgeois ethos of restriction through pretension, the voluntaristic rigour of the 'called' but not yet 'chosen'" (Bourdieu 1979 [2004]: 339; italics in original). The dominant class achieves the distinction which creates distance by dint of the very fact that "one is not seeking distinction, seeking to be different; 'truly distinguished' people are those who do not care about distinction" (Bourdieu 1989b: 18). As a rule this provides them with an unbeatable advantage in terms of access to exclusive educational institutions and positions of social power.

In his book *Distinction. A Social Critique of the Judgement of Taste* Bourdieu characterizes the effects of habitus as follows:

> In a whole host of markets, from the major state examinations to editor-ial boards, from job interviews to garden parties, the cultural produc-tions of the petit-bourgeois habitus are subtly discredited because they recall their acquisition in matters in which, more than anywhere else, the important thing is to know without ever having learnt . . . The petit bourgeois do not know how to play the game of culture as a game. They take culture too seriously to go in for bluff or imposture or even for the distance and casualness which show true familiarity; too seriously to escape permanent fear of ignorance or blunders, or to sidestep tests by responding with the indifference of those who are not competing or the serene detachment of those who feel entitled to confess or even flaunt their lacunae.
>
> (Bourdieu 1979 [2004]: 330)

The reproduction strategies of the dominant class, aimed as they are rein-forcing its position, are rooted in this difference. Essentially, Bourdieu notes, strategies are nothing more than an anticipation of the future based on past experience. They are determined by objective capital endowments as well as by expectations, hopes, and action perspectives (in the form of habitus) that have been shaped by the past. The frequently observed, very close correlation between subjective expectations and objective probabilities is thus not the result of an individual's precise assessment of his chances of success, it is due, rather, to the fact that the most improbable practices are eliminated by habitus, itself an important factor in the objective conditions concerned (Bourdieu 1980 [1990]: 54). Habitus is primarily guided by the signals it is tuned to perceive, signals that are directly related to the past internalized in it. In contrast to widespread belief, strategies are, then, mostly of an unconscious nature and are objectively keyed, in the form of ordered actions, to goals which, as Bourdieu points out at one stage, need not necessarily be the ones subjectively aimed for. "The strategies I am talking about are actions objectively oriented towards goals that may not be the goals subjectively pursued" (Bourdieu 1993a: 76). The objective homogenization of class habitus, originating as it does from the homogeneity of given conditions of existence, ensures that, despite all conflicts, countless individual practices and strategies harmonize with one another. In this way they contribute incessantly to reproducing the given social structure (Bourdieu and Wacquant 1992: 140).[12]

Because of their habitus attachment, strategies are invariably most successful – i.e. optimally adapted to a given situation – when current conditions are the same as or similar to the conditions under which a habitus was formed.[13] Accordingly, the greatest danger involved in rapid or profound changes in conditions is that a person may not be able to behave adequately in a particular new situation, the reason being that a habitus based in part on outdated experiences is not able to adapt quickly enough. However, Bourdieu continues, this danger is relatively small. While thought and behavior patterns generated by past experiences do shape perceptions of existing situations and the actions derived from them, there is nothing automatic about the process; habitus can of course "at every moment, structure new experiences in accordance with the structures produced by past experiences" (Bourdieu 1980 [1990]: 60). While it does favor certain reactions, there is no immediate constraint involved. Although everyone prefers approaches that correspond most closely to the dispositions determined by his past, and habitus is thus characterized by its relatively closed nature, it still remains open in that "habitus reveals itself . . . only in reference to a definite situation" (Bourdieu and Wacquant 1992: 135). Bourdieu goes on to argue that we perceive situations from the perspective of the earlier experiences internalized in our habitus, although as a rule we are obliged to react more or less positively to concrete situations and to major changes, that is, to react by adapting our own habitus to new conditions. Thus habitus is not characterized once and for all by wholly specific features (e.g. particular dress or behavior) or specific tastes (for example, in painting or in music). Dogged insistence on outdated behavior patterns, and the failure which inevitably results – one might think of Cervantes' "Don Quixote" in this connection – remain the exception.

Today education is the one sector of society that plays a particularly strong role in the reproduction strategies of individuals and classes, and in which changes in these strategies are especially clearly manifest. If the dominant class is forced by economic restructuring to attach major, indeed in many cases even crucial, importance to the possession of higher academic qualifications in filling positions of power, thus according less significance to direct inheritance, this necessary change in the dominant class' reproduction strategies is in many respects facilitated and fostered by its habitus as well as by the capital available to it.

With regard to strategies for investment in education, Bourdieu notes that, generally speaking, the risk of misinvestment is considerably higher for members of the lower and middle classes. In the first place, they are not familiar enough with the institutions of the education and employment system to be able to correctly assess future developments and hence the value of certain academic qualifications; and second, they do not have sufficient economic and cultural capital to be able to wait for uncertain returns to investment or to be able to choose the more risky but often more prestigious path (Bourdieu 1974 [1981]: 179). Furthermore, educational institutions themselves are at pains to select only "predisposed" actors. There are, for instance, institutions in which "little more is expected of students than that they be themselves, that is, demonstrate the attitudes and skills (behavior, accent, stance, etc.) which are the legacy of their class of origin." Since purely technical skills would never be sufficient for a position as manager of a corporation or as a distinguished physician, and since the overall habitus that goes along with such positions is likewise important, educational institutions tend to select predisposed habituses and to superimpose "on this selection effects of rupture, of closure, of consecration, which are crucial for the inheritors to take over their inheritance" (Bourdieu 1993b: 32).

All these factors, Bourdieu holds, are particularly apparent with respect to admission to the most renowned educational institutions, e.g. to the famous Grandes écoles such as ENA, Polytechnique, and HEC, or the similarly exclusive Sciences Po. The principle function of these elite universities, whose exclusive character has remained untouched by the expansion of education due to their specific structures and strict admission conditions, is to produce an elite generally accepted by society.[14] Their alumni represent, both in their own eyes and in the eyes of the general public, the "elite's elite." And thus degrees from these institutions are becoming increasingly indispensable for top positions and are more and more taking on the character, even in large corporations, and in particular in those without majority private ownership, of an *"entry pass"* (285; italics in original) to the top echelons of management (Bourdieu 1989a [1996]: 285, 308–9).[15]

To ensure that the reproduction of the dominant class is guaranteed by the need to acquire these exclusive academic titles, though, the Grandes écoles have to demonstrate the necessary degree of social selectivity. As Bourdieu shows in a study on the background of students and graduates, there is no doubt that this is the case (ibid.: 137–8, 169, 246–8). The overwhelming majority of students at the Grandes écoles are in fact offspring of the dominant class. The principle reason for this heavily disproportionate bias is, according to Bourdieu, the similarity or structural rapport between the requirements of these elite educational institutions and the habitus of applicants from the dominant class. This applies in two different ways. First, the selections made by the responsible faculty are influenced in key ways by a habitus-related affinity vis-à-vis candidates from the upper middle classes or the upper class. This serves to create sympathy. Second, the very behavior of these candidates suggests they should be admitted, whereas others exclude themselves, as it were, spontaneously (ibid.: 141).

In her analysis of the French aristocracy, de Saint Martin quotes ENA examination reports which cast light on this dual effect. To quote:

> The examination interview does not serve to test the candidate's knowledge . . . [It is rather] a methodical attempt to appraise human qualities at an age at which people are not yet able to properly dissimulate . . . A member of the examination committee once said, "I try to imagine whether I would like to work with the candidate I am listening to, and whether I would trust him or her completely." In other words, the emphasis is on the human personality, and not some being armed with diplomas and book knowledge. Being able to admit to gaps in one's knowledge, having a casual but not arrogant attitude, the gift of showing presence of mind in one's replies, and intellectual curiosity are [seen as] excellent characteristics.
>
> (de Saint Martin 1993: 203)

It is impossible to overlook the way in which these desirable traits harmonize with the habitus of the dominant class. Even so, Bourdieu argues, the path through these exclusive educational institutions does curtail the "power of the family," that is:

> the power to single out from the total of all children belonging to a particular cohort and coming from the same social class those children who are destined to reproduce their class with all its features, or who are to be excluded from this class.
>
> (Bourdieu and de Saint Martin 1978: 23)

Whereas in the traditional system of inheritance this decision was wholly in the hands of the family, the family is now obliged to bow to the rules of the education system as a field in its own right. In statistical terms, the effect remains the same: the reproduction of the dominant class in general is just as secure in this case as when power is handed down directly; it is the principles of selection that are different. Educational institutions, it is argued, can only make their contribution to reproduction if they follow their own rules, i.e. if they are prepared to sacrifice individual dominant-class children who would have been "spared" under a reproduction mechanism fully controlled by the family (Bourdieu 1989a [1996]: 287; Bourdieu and de Saint Martin 1978: 25).

However, this loss of direct influence is, Bourdieu contends, mitigated by the fact that academic titles are neither necessary nor sufficient prerequisites for all dominant positions. On the one hand, the traditional mechanisms by which power is transferred continue to be very important in companies that are still predominantly family-owned, even though this is becoming less and less the case and company heirs are finding themselves increasingly compelled to present more prestigious academic qualifications. On the other hand, a diploma from one of the famous Grandes écoles is not as a rule sufficient on its own to capture top positions, even in large state-owned enterprises or in companies not under the control of private shareholders. There, too, the key is generally the right parental background, i.e. one must come from the ranks of the dominant class. This is clearly illustrated by the social background of the top managers in these companies (Bourdieu 1989a [1996]: 288–9, 306, 310).

Moreover, the new mode of reproduction has one inestimable advantage over the old: its statistical effectiveness alone goes a long way toward masking the real power mechanisms in operation. Since the anonymous "concours" in principle gives everyone the same chances,[16] and since there are always new examples of people who have reached the top of large corporations without the "right" background, the effectiveness of this mode of reproducing the dominant class is not apparent on the surface. This provides for a high degree of legitimacy. And this in turn affects the self-image of the new business elite. "Convinced that its own legitimacy stems not from wealth or birth, but from 'intelligence' and 'competence,' the business nobility perceives itself as an enlightened avant-garde, able to conceive, desire, and direct the change necessary to 'conserve' [power]" (Bourdieu 1989a [1996]: 320).[17]

All in all, Bourdieu notes, there have been few dominant groups in history that have had so many and so varied principles to legitimize their power as the top ranks of the French bourgeoisie. These persons are in the position to invoke family descent and academic achievement, the ideology of "public service," and the cult of profit and productivity. Consisting almost exclusively of the major Parisian families, bankers, industrialists, top civil servants, and high-level judges, among whom – by dint of "vocations" and cooptation – the important positions of power are distributed,[18] they tend, in all fields, to maintain a power which resembles the power over economic capital, i.e. a power that results from their ability to mobilize financial capital (ibid.: 335).

Bourdieu sees the Grandes écoles fulfilling another important role beside the reproduction of the dominant class as a whole. By virtue of the fact that there are various types of Grande école (from the schools such as ENS that focus on the arts to the HEC with its clear orientation toward the economic sciences) these schools solve a second central problem, namely the internal structuring of this class. Both the practice of cooptation by teaching staff who have themselves attended a Grande école and the fact of their varied appeal to the different groups of the dominant class mean that each of the different Grandes écoles provides for a high degree of social homogeneity (ibid.: 181–7). It is important in this context that the struggles between the two major segments, the ruling faction, which is dominated by economic capital, and the ruled faction, with its mainly cultural capital, are deprived of some of their severity when they are channeled in the right directions.[19] The arrangement in effect at the Grandes écoles are, Bourdieu notes, equivalent to the arrangements for succession from former days, which aimed to prevent fratricidal struggles over succession between heirs (Bourdieu 1993b: 22). In this respect as well, then, the structures of the education system ensure that the dominant class is reproduced.

4.3 Summary

The theoretical approaches of Mills and Bourdieu concur in two central points. Both agree that there is not a large number of interdependent sub-elites of generally equal standing, asserting instead that what we find is a single power elite or ruling class which, despite its internal differentiation (which both see), is marked by strong internal cohesion and dominated by the owning, or ruling, class, and above all by the faction of the dominant class that is endowed with economic capital. Mills and Bourdieu also both see the principle foundation of this cohesion in an identical or at least similar family and school socialization of members of the power elite or dominant class. They thus contradict the functionalist assumption that the meritocratic principle has opened access to the elite for all social groups. Furthermore, both Mills and Bourdieu, unlike most functionalist theorists, focus relatively sharply on the relationship between the power elite or dominant class and the other classes or strata of society as well as on the historical changes they have undergone. This can be seen particularly clearly in Mills' work, where he breaks down the position of US elites into various historical phases, especially in his analysis of the New Deal (Mills 1959: 259–68), as well as in his depiction of the social conditions requisite to the rise of multimillionaires like Carnegie or Rockefeller (ibid.: 97–101). Indeed, it can be said that comparisons between the different classes of society run through just about everything Bourdieu wrote. The differences between these classes are the factor that shapes both his early work on educational sociology and his later studies on habitus and power.

Irrespective of this extensive common ground, there are substantial differences between Mills and Bourdieu both in their approaches to the central issues concerned and in their individual analyses. While Mills is principally interested in the question of how and by whom core decisions affecting society at large are made, Bourdieu focuses his attention primarily on the mechanisms responsible for the reproduction of the dominant class and its power. This distinction then also gives shape to the individual stages and results of his studies.

Three examples may serve to illustrate this point. Mills, for instance, is explicitly concerned with the manner in which the mass forms and formulates its political will. What he finds is: widespread unknowledgeability, uniformity, and passivity, all due in essence to the mass's disinterest in "participation in public life" and the manipulative power of the mass media, which are controlled by the power elite.[20] Bourdieu, in contrast, does not devote nearly as much attention to this issue and is far less instrumental in his arguments regarding the process of the formation of broad public opinion and the role of the mass media. At the forefront of his interest are the habitus-related mechanisms used by the ruled classes to adapt "voluntarily" to given social conditions. Bourdieu explicitly derives the fact that the ruled show more subordination (and less subversion and resistance) from the logic involved in adapting dispositions to given conditions (Bourdieu and Wacquant 1992 [1996]: 111). Accordingly, terms such as "terrorized" or "intimidated" masses, which are not hard to find in Mills, are wholly absent in Bourdieu's works.

Mills also sees the role of smaller self-employed persons in a different light. While Bourdieu views the lower middle classes exclusively from the angle of their (generally) futile attempts to ascend into the ranks of the dominant class, describing both these efforts and the overall petty-bourgeois habitus in unambiguous terms, indeed often even with biting irony, Mills has a certain tendency to idealize, at least in historical retrospect. In his view, the old middle class represented the last bastion against the advance of large organizations and, ultimately, the victory of the power elite – the last independent force with a power basis of its own. With this class, he asserts, both of one of the most important – if not indeed the most important – national foundations of a relative balance of political power and the power of the classic professional politician in US government and administration have disappeared from the scene once and for all.

Finally, Mills places far greater emphasis than Bourdieu on the direct interests and projects of the power elite. While he expressly rejects conspiracy theories and stresses the central significance of structural conditions (organizational interests, origins, cooperation), he also accords attention to the personal desires of the members of the power elite as well as to their strategic projects. He even goes so far as to speak of plots directly forged by this elite. While its rise to power was not achieved on the basis of such plots, it was instrumental in formulating projects, programs, and, above all, organizational structures like the National Security Council, the existence of which, he asserts, is certainly not the result of the normal workings of the major national institutions in the economic, political, and military sectors. Although the power elite normally uses existing organizational structures to push through its own projects, certain "more far-sighted" members of the elite make use of the opportunities their positions offer to create new organizations, the advantages of which become evident only much later, even to most other members of the elite (ibid.: 292–3). Bourdieu's overall line of argument, on the other hand, is focused on mechanisms that operate subliminally. In his view the dominant class is always at its most effective in the pursuit of its goals when its actions emerge largely unconsciously from its habitus. Bourdieu even criticizes, for instance, social scientists like Edward P. Thompson (to whom he attributes a particular sensitivity for symbolic effects) for their inclination to believe that symbolic practices such as pompous robes or powdered wigs were "explicit strategies of domination intended to be seen (from below) and to interpret generous or charitable conducts as 'calculated acts of class appeasement.'"[21] And yet it may be precisely "that the most sincerely disinterested acts may be those best corresponding to objective interest" (Bourdieu 1983 [1997]: 57).

Differences between Mills and Bourdieu are also evident where they deal with the role of social background and educational institutions. While Bourdieu places the significance of class-specific habitus and official academic qualifications at the center of his argument, Mills accords greater weight to internal organizational mechanisms, that is, to nonfamily and nonscholastic socialization processes. This is less true of the business sector, where, in Mills' opinion, people are chiefly reliant for advancement on the sympathy of their superiors, whose expectations they must meet and whose confidence they must win. All this is easiest for those who have "started from on high, because they have from their beginnings been formed by sound men and trained for soundness" (Mills 1959: 140–6). This, however, is different in the case of the military. Here, parental background and associated personal attributes play a smaller role in filling top positions. These are "far less important" for higher-ranking officers than for others in top positions of society because the military world is so "all-inclusive" that it "dominates" one's entire life. The military constitutes a "caste;" the social background of members of the military should not be underestimated in looking at military recruitment and action, but it is important not to lose sight of the fact that the military sector is far more autonomous, i.e. subject to laws of its own, than, for instance, the business sector (ibid.: 192–7).

Apart from the above-described similarities and differences, the theoretical approaches of Mills and Bourdieu also have one common weakness. Although in numerous formulations both accord the ruling class or the dominant faction of the ruling class a pre-eminent position within the power elite or ruling class, in the end their lines of argumentation remain more or less vague. At first sight it is evident that both authors focus their analyses on the owners and top executives of large corporations. In the "Power Elite" Mills devotes almost twice as much space to them as he does to the political and military elite together, and Bourdieu deals less intensively with this class or class faction and its reproduction strategies than he does with the segment of the dominant class whose position is rooted primarily in ownership of economic capital.

This first superficial impression is further reinforced when we take a closer look at the development of their lines of argumentation. Not only does Mills attribute the uniformity of the power elite to its common origin in the propertied class, he also describes in considerable detail the great extent to which important political positions are filled by representatives of big industry. Although he repeatedly points to the intertwinement of the three sectors business, politics, and the military, in his actual analysis he focuses almost exclusively on examples that serve to illustrate the direct influence of the business elite on politics or to depict its direct ascent into high political office. He furthermore speaks of cliques consisting of the leading men of industry who, without having to play much of a role as actual members of the political or military leadership, are still "in on most major decisions regardless of topic" (ibid.: 292). In view of all these statements it is not surprising to see Mills refer to the "chief executives who sit in the political directorate" as "those who, by fact and by proxy, hold the power and the means." Put in a nutshell, what he is saying is: "If they do not reign, they do govern at many of the vital points of everyday life in America ..." There are, he states, "no powers [that] effectively and consistently countervail against them" (ibid.: 125).

Such drastic remarks are not to be found in Bourdieu's work. However, in many of his writings, particularly those published before the end of the 1980s, he does speak of the dominant role of economic capital and its owners. He makes his position particularly clear in the essay which most systematically sets out his theory of capital. Here he states:

> So it has to be posited simultaneously that economic capital is at the root of all the other types of capital and that these transformed, disguised forms of economic capital, never entirely reducible to that definition, produce their most specific effects only to the extent that they conceal (not least form their possessors) the fact that economic capital is at their root, in other words – but only in the last analysis – at the root of their effects.
>
> (Bourdieu 1983 [1997]: 54)

This statement, certain elements of which (e.g. the term 'in the last analysis') are very reminiscent of Marx, accords well with what he has to say about the dominant faction of the ruling class. Bourdieu likewise explains this faction's dominance over the ruled faction of intellectuals and artists in terms of the various amounts of economic capital they have at their disposal. In his more recent writings he also concedes that "obviously, in advanced capitalist societies, it would be difficult to maintain that the economic field does not exercise especially powerful determinations" (Bourdieu and Wacquant 1992: 109).

On the other hand, both Mills and Bourdieu repeatedly and explicitly criticize the assumption that there is such a thing as a power hierarchy with the business elite at its top. Both take a firm stand against any simplified economism which directly equates economic power with political rule.[22]

Mills, for whom this is a reason to entirely avoid using the term ruling class, points in his criticism primarily to the degree of autonomy which has to be ascribed to political and military elites. Judging by the way he depicts political decision-making structures, he must have been thinking chiefly of the military. In his opinion, the military's power has grown considerably as a result of the world-political situation and the potentials of modern weapons systems, and he sees the military's level of power as extremely high. However, his study contains no precise definition of the overall power relations between the three subelites. In view of his own analysis of the social origins of the power elite and the extent of the influence which the business elite has on the making of political decisions, his reference to the autonomy of politics and the military is not sufficient to clarify this issue. In the end, his statements on the role played by the owning class and the business elite in the constitution and the actions of the power elite leave a good number of questions unanswered.

The thrust of Bourdieu's thinking is a different one. From the very beginning he is critical for example of Sartre's myth of the free intellectual as the "opponent of any and all power" (Bourdieu 1992: 41), that is, he criticizes in particular the view that the critical stance taken by numerous intellectuals toward the owners of large companies or (more generally) toward big economic capital constitutes any fundamental antagonism. Clearly influenced by the events of May 1968, he sees in such strife no more than a conflict between the two factions of the dominant class over their respective share of power. Ultimately, Bourdieu argues, the conflict between the two factions of the dominant class "fosters a form of complementarity which is the basis of a veritable *organic solidarity within the division of labour of domination*. Thus," Bourdieu goes on, "the couple of those who act and those who speak is at once antagonistic and complementary" (Bourdieu 1993b: 25; italics in original).

Many revolutions, he notes unequivocally, are "exclusively revolutions within the dominant class," adding that these are concerned with nothing other than the value of individual types of capital in given situations. As in a game, everything centers in essence around deciding "whether one chip of 'economic capital' is really worth three chips of 'cultural capital'" (ibid.: 38). However, this approach in essence leaves open the question of the actual power relations between the two factions of the dominant class; and there is no reason to assume that the dominated faction might not itself one day become the dominant one. It would be entirely conceivable for the intellectuals to supplant those whose power is based chiefly on the possession of economic capital.

Beginning in the late 1980s, however, Bourdieu goes a step further. In *La Noblesse d'Etat* he explicitly rejects the term dominant class in favor of "field of power." His reason for doing so is, he states, his need to "break with all existing theories" about the dominant class because they, regardless of all differences, have one thing in common: they study populations of power players rather than the structures of power (Bourdieu 1993b: 20). This certainly applies for many approaches in elite research, but whether or not it can justifiably be asserted at this level of generality is more than questionable. When, in one of his last major publications, Bourdieu seeks to explain his use of the term "field of power," he notes that:

> domination is not the direct and simple action exercised by a set of agents ("the dominant class") invested with powers of coercion. Rather, it is the indirect effect of a complex set of actions engendered within the network of intersecting constraints which each of the dominants, thus dominated by the structure of the field through which domination is exerted, endures on behalf of all the others.
>
> (Bourdieu 1994 [1998]: 34)

This is a formulation that is more than extremely complicated. Reduction, albeit indirectly, of the dominant class to a group of actors who actually hold and exert coercive power may be justified as a critical comment on many analyses of elites which use this term, but it is not applicable for example to Mills, and certainly not to his own older publications that operate with the term dominant class. Bourdieu's core arguments on the position of the various classes in relation to one another and the central significance of the possession of the various types of capital for one's own position in social space are all unambiguously stated there. The approach of *La Noblesse d'Etat*, which simply adopts some important sections from earlier studies (sometimes verbatim), simply altering their terminology, would not otherwise have been possible. All in all, it is difficult to see what advantages are gained by these terminological amendments.

However, the difficulties into which this leads Bourdieu are plain to see. This goes for one point in particular. Bourdieu does not really succeed in drawing a clear line between the field of power and state power. He does point out explicitly that the field of power should not be confused with the political field (Bourdieu 1994 [1998]: 34), but at the same time he states unmistakably that the historical concentration of the different types of capital have led to the emergence of state capital, a "kind of *meta-capital*." It is this that permits the state to "wield power over the different fields and over the various forms of capital" as well as over their relative currency with respect to one another. The "construction of the state consequently goes hand in hand with the construction of the field of power." The latter should be understood as the space in which the various owners of capital "struggle *in particular* for power over the state, that is, over the statist capital that grants power over the different species of capital and over their reproduction (via the school system in particular)" (Bourdieu and Wacquant 1992: 114; original italics). It is impossible to overlook the fact that what he has in mind here is the French system, with its (by international comparison) considerable state influence and its Grandes écoles.[23] At the very least, the weakening of the structures of the nation-state as a result of globalization and the rapidly progressing internationalization of the economy has placed a question mark over any such marked focus on the state. For the same reason it would, conversely, appear essential to place greater emphasis on the economic field, and, to use Bourdieu's words, the power of the top executives of large multinational corporations.

Questions

1   What does Mills understand by the "power elite"?
2   How does Mills explain the relationship between the military, the political, and the business elite?
3   How does Mills characterize the mass society?
4   What is the difference between the two reproduction strategies of the "dominant faction of the ruling class" in Bourdieu?
5   Which part do the cultural and the economic capital play in the reproduction process?
6   How does Bourdieu define the "habitus"?

5 National education systems and elite recruitment

All leading industrialized nations, with the exception of Germany, have specific elite educational institutions behind the walls of which the key social elites spend the decisive years of their school and/or university education. Regardless of whether these are public or private institutions, schools or universities, their function is always the same. The degrees obtained from these elite educational institutions are one of the main keys to accessing top positions in business, administration, politics, law, and academia, and they at the same time ensure that the process of social selection favors upper middle- and upper-class children. In France this role falls primarily to the renowned elite universities, the Grandes écoles such as the ENA or the École Polytechnique; in Great Britain the same role is played by the famous public schools such as Eton or Winchester and the distinguished universities of Oxford and Cambridge; in the US it is the renowned private universities such as Harvard, Yale, or Princeton; and the scene in Japan is dominated by the five most respected elite universities, headed by the state Imperial University of Tokyo, commonly known as Todai.

5.1 France: the Grandes écoles and the Grands Corps

The Grandes écoles, some of which were founded before the French Revolution, are the traditional elite universities of the French education system. Taken together, they train no more than some 100,000 of a total of 2.2 million students. However, only a small number of these universities, with no more than a few thousand students, play a really important role in training the country's future elites. The diplomas most in demand for recruitment to the highest positions are awarded by the four most famous Grandes écoles, the administrative cadre training school, ENA (École Nationale d'Administration), the engineering-oriented École Polytechnique, the school of economic sciences, HEC (Hautes Études Commerciales), and the liberal arts schools, ENS (Écoles Normales Supérieures).

These universities accept only a few hundred students each year. Last year, for example, 116 students were accepted for the ENA, 380 for the HEC, and 400 for the École Polytechnique. With the exception of the HEC, which is operated by the Paris Chamber of Commerce and charges fees of almost €15,000 (half for tuition, half for room and board), these are all state institutions which pay their civil service candidates a monthly salary of between €991 (ENS) and €1,220 (ENA) for the duration of their studies. Since the number of places available at these universities has remained largely static for decades, and the selection process is correspondingly strict (only 5 to 10 percent of applicants pass the entrance examinations), the Grandes écoles have remained untouched by the general expansion in the field of university education. While at present a good two-thirds of any one cohort are awarded the baccalaureat, which qualifies students to attend a university, and almost all of them then go on to study, a fact which has led to a tenfold increase in the number of students over the last 40 years, very little has changed in the Grandes écoles, and they have been able to retain their exclusive character.

This exclusiveness is also reflected in the social composition of their student bodies. The following figures, which indicate the social backgrounds of students in the so-called *classes préparatoires*[1] and students at the Grandes écoles over the last three decades, demonstrate how slight the chances are of a working-class or middle-class child passing through the various selection filters installed upstream of the Grandes écoles. At the end of the 1970s, 50 to 60 percent of such students already came from the higher strata of society (Marceau 1977: 108). At that time the HEC was the most exclusive in terms of social recruitment, with approximately 80 percent of its students coming from families of entrepreneurs, professionals, executives, and higher-level civil servants. This was followed by the ENA, with about 75 percent, and the École Polytechnique, with about 71.5 percent (Bourdieu 1989a: 192).

In subsequent decades this blatant disparity in the composition of student bodies has even widened somewhat. Today the proportion of working-class children in the *classes préparatoires* is only 6.8 percent, while *cadres supérieures* and *professeurs* account for about 48.5 percent. Working-class and middle-class children in the broader sense have also lost ground at the leading Grandes écoles. Between 1960 and 1970 approximately 21.2 percent of students at the four most renowned Grandes écoles came from an *origine populaire* (farmers, workers, lower- and middle-level salaried employees and civil servants, self-employed tradesmen, and business people), but between 1989 and 1993 this figure had fallen to only 8.6 percent. The number of children from families of *cadres supérieures* and *professeurs* rose in the same period by about one-fifth to almost 80 percent (Euriat and Thélot 1995: 410, 434–6). It is particularly interesting to note how marked the process of social selection is in the case of the ENA, even though over 50 percent of the candidates are graduates of the other Grandes écoles and the selection process involved is quite complex. Only one in ten children from upper-middle and upper-class backgrounds, who accounted for about two-thirds of applicants between 1983 and 1985, passed the entrance examination; only one in 20 of the one-third of applicants who came from working-class or lower middle-class backgrounds passed the examinations (Bourdieu 1989a [1966]: 366).[2]

All in all, this social selection must be seen as a process involving different several stages. It begins with the highly disparate proportion of children from the various social classes and strata that acquire the baccalaureat. While only one in five working-class children earn this diploma, the figure is four in five for children of executives, members of the free professions, and higher-level teaching staff. The second crucial obstacle must be seen in the choice of a type of baccalaureat. If we look at Baccalaureat C,[3] with its mathematical–scientific focus – and it is chosen by less than 16 percent of all pupils taking the baccalaureat – we find that – compared with the average school diploma – its acquisition raises fivefold the chances applicants have of passing the entrance examination. Bac-C, on the other hand, is chosen by a far above-average proportion of upper-class children. While the share of children of executives, higher-level civil servants, and professionals taking the less prestigious Bacs F and G is only about 14 percent, as opposed to approximately 40 percent for children of normal white- and blue-collar workers, the ratio in the case of Bac-C is almost exactly the reverse: 48 percent as opposed to only 19 percent (Kerviel 1991: 40–2; Roulin-Lefebvre and Esquieu 1992: 6).

Even though tuition fees are still the exception, and although the use of standardized examinations for the selection process appears at first sight to offer the same chances of success to all, the French education system still provides for an extremely efficient social selection. There is one central reason for this "efficiency." Upper middle-class and upper class families are generally better endowed with the means needed to overcome the various selection barriers than are families from the other classes and strata. As a rule they have both the economic and the cultural resources needed to provide their children with a crucial head start in acquiring the knowledge required for the examinations. Furthermore, high self-recruitment rates due to selection by the staff of the renowned lycées and, above all, the Grandes écoles, where the rate is as high as 90 percent, clearly favor those who come from the same high strata of society as these faculty members and thus share, or are at least well acquainted with, their language, tastes, and manners (Bourdieu and Passeron 1964 [1979]). The statement made by an ENA examiner on his selection criteria and quoted in Chapter 4 (de Saint Martin 1993: 203) is more than a good illustration of the significance of social background and associated habitus for admission to one of the renowned Grandes écoles.

The door to careers in all important sectors of society is open to anyone who has taken a degree at one of the renowned Grandes écoles. The most successful of them are the graduates of the ENA, the so-called Enarques. They tend to be predominant not only in top positions in politics, administration, and administrative justice but also in many large corporations. A brief look at the French presidents and prime ministers over the last 30 years shows how dominant the political position of these persons has become over recent decades. Two of France's recent presidents (Giscard d'Estaing and Chirac) and six of 11 prime ministers have been ENA alumni. In addition, three other prime ministers had attended one of the other Grandes écoles. Only two of this total of 11 were without an exclusive diploma of this kind. We see a similar picture on the ministerial level, where two of Prime Minister Raffarin's four key ministries (foreign affairs and justice) are headed by Enarques and one by a Polytechnicien.

The situation in France's political administration is basically similar, if not quite as blatant. Of the members of the *cabinets ministeriels*, the personal staffs of French ministers, 18.8 percent were Enarques even under Socialist Prime Minister Rocard (1988–1991). Under his conservative successors, Balladur and Juppé, this figure rose to 36 and then to 38 percent. The bias in favor of ENA graduates is even more pronounced in the case of the ministerial directors who head these cabinets. Already at the beginning of the 1980s, 37 percent were ENA graduates. By the middle of the 1990s this figure had increased to 70 percent, a rise from approximately one in three to almost three in four. The Enarques are also dominant in other administrative sectors. One of every two directors of the other ministries, for instance, is an Enarque. The case is the same for two of every three prefects, one of every two ambassadors, and four of every five judges in France's supreme administrative court (the Conseil d'Etat).

The above clearly illustrates that the Enarques occupy a large share of the positions in the Grands Corps, the elite institutions of public administration in which a large number of France's highest-level civil servants are employed. Traditionally, the ten to 15 best ENA graduates of each year are able to choose between the three most important nontechnical Grands Corps (Conseil d'Etat, Cour des Comptes, and Inspection des Finances), and they occupy between two-thirds and four-fifths of all positions there. In the remaining high ranks of civil administration they account for 69 percent, the corresponding figure for the diplomatic corps being one-third (Bock 1999: 390–6; Chevallier 1997: 92; Kesler 1997: 25–7; Suleiman 1997: 39). If we also take into account the fact that the 50 to 60 best graduates of the École Polytechnique are equally well represented in the most important technical Grands Corps (Corps des Mines and Corps des Ponts et Chausées), the dominant role of the Grandes écoles in French politics becomes more than clear.

The picture is no different at the top levels of business. Of the managing directors (PDGs) of the 200 largest French corporations, 57 percent have studied at the ENA, the École Polytechnique or the HEC. Despite its focus on the economic sciences, the private HEC, with its share of only around 7 percent, lags far behind its two state-run rivals, each of which accounts for almost 25 percent. Of the 100 largest French corporations, more than two-thirds are run by graduates of these three universities, 30 of them Enarques, another 30 Polytechniciens, and 10 HEC graduates. Enarques are predominant in the financial sector, where they run 13 of the 20 top companies, and

Polytechniciens are highly in evidence in industry, where they hold 21 of 50 top executive positions. The enormous influence of this handful of elite institutions on the way in which top management positions are filled becomes even clearer when we look at the percentage of Grandes écoles graduates who have subsequently found positions within one of the renowned Grands Corps. Seventy-two of France's 200 major corporations – and 40 of its 100 largest – are run by former Grands Corps members (Bauer and Bertin-Mourot 1996: 48–50; Hartmann 2000: 246–7).

This enormous concentration of power in the hands of a small elite circle of Grandes école graduates is particularly evident when we view it in the context defined by the percentage for which this group accounts in the population as a whole. With just 500 graduates a year, that is 0.6 per mill of a cohort, between them the ENA and the École Polytechnique supply the majority of top positions in French society. A large share of these positions is filled by an even smaller circle, that is, by the roughly 80 students who are recruited by the Grand Corps when they graduate. This amounts to 0.1 per mill of a cohort.

This massive quantitative restriction goes hand in hand with a strict social selection. For instance, two of three French presidents and four of 11 prime ministers have come from the upper class, the top 0.5 per mill of society, while only three have come from working-class and lower middle-class backgrounds, the bottom 96.5 percent of society. The rest have stemmed from upper middle-class backgrounds.[4] Top executives are no exception here. Of the PDGs of France's 100 largest corporations, almost 50 percent grew up in upper-class surroundings and another 40 percent in middle-class families. By comparison, only one in nine are recruited from the broad population. The administrative sector presents a similarly clear-cut, if not quite so extreme, picture. Two-thirds of the members of the most distinguished Grands Corps and almost half of all other high-ranking civil servants stem from the upper middle classes. Almost three-quarters of these are graduates of the ENA or another Grande école, far outdistancing all others (Rouban 1999: 79–81). In summary, it can be said that the offspring of the upper middle classes remain largely among themselves when it comes to filling society's top positions.

The commonalities that result from a shared or at least similar social background are even further intensified by these persons' exclusive education and training. A very marked esprit de corps is a feature common to former Grandes écoles students and (even more) to members of the Grands Corps. To begin with, this esprit comes automatically from a sense of belonging to a small elite and is thus the logical expression of the elite status of the Grandes écoles or the Grands Corps as well as of the long path that students traverse together in earning a qualification from one of these institutions. This common ground makes its mark across the board, ignoring party or sectoral boundaries. It creates a sense of shared understanding and trust, but it also fosters favoritism and corruption, as numerous court cases involving the top levels of French society have recently shown.

The consciousness of belonging to the "chosen few" is furthermore systematically fostered by the Grandes écoles and their alumni. For instance, it is customary for the alumni of the École Polytechnique, irrespective of their professional position, to call each other *camarade* and to be available to one another at any time, even for concrete mutual support. An example from the late 1960s demonstrates just how far this mechanism extends. The then president of the ENS in Paris terminated his friendship with Prime Minister Pompidou as an alumni of this institution because the latter had refused to stop criminal proceedings against a left-wing ENS student, Alain Geismar, for allegedly wrongfully killing a policeman. For the university president, the fact that Pompidou placed raison d'etat higher than camaraderie among members of the ENS was an unpardonable offense. The ties among members of the Grands Corps, above all of the renowned "Corps des Mines," "Corps des Ponts et Chausées," "Inspection des Finances" are even closer. They make for marked preferential treatment in the filling of top positions, thus ensuring the great weight of and continuity of the influence wielded by corps members in all sectors of society.

5.2 The UK: Eton and Oxbridge

In the UK exclusive educational institutions are likewise the crucial narrow gate to access to the country's important elites. In contrast to France, however, this crucial role is played less by the universities – although Oxford and Cambridge are two decidedly elite institutions – than by a number of highly prestigious private schools which form the core of the 200 so-called public schools recognized and listed by the Headmasters' Conference (HMC). At the top of this list are the so-called Clarendon Nine, the nine oldest and most prestigious British public schools, including Eton, Winchester, and Harrow. Together with a further 20 top schools, they make up the "Eton and Rugby Groups" which are attended by only 0.5 per mill of a cohort.

These schools are, almost without exception, boarding schools, and thus school provides the backdrop to almost all aspects of students' day-to-day lives. Since these students have frequently attended private preparatory schools, also organized on a boarding basis, from the age of seven to 13, and sometimes also preparatory schools for five- to seven-year-olds, the attitudes and behavior of upper-class children – that is, children from the top 1 percent of society – are molded to a far greater extent by their schools than is the case in France. This means, then, that transmission within the family context of habitus and education is of lesser importance to admission to the country's elite educational institutions. While it is true that public school students must show considerable intellectual potential and the right "habitus" if they are to pass the difficult entrance examinations in English, French, mathematics, history, geography, and several other optional subjects, financial endowments play a much larger and also more direct role than is the case in France. Those who wish to send their children to a public school must, first and foremost, be in a position to pay huge school fees of up to £19,100 per year. Since the average annual income in the UK, below £20,000, lies roughly in the same range, and since scholarships are the exception, these schools remain effectively closed to the broad population.

A glance at all the HMC schools illustrates the degree of social selectivity practiced by these schools, which on average cost only half as much as Eton, Winchester, or Westminster. For decades now, some 90 percent of their students have come from the so-called service class, which is made up of the top fifth of British society, and two-thirds of students come from Service Class I, which includes only about 5 percent of the population (Edwards *et al.* 1989: 162). Their parents' incomes are thus two or three times higher than the average. At famous public schools like Eton or Harrow, social recruitment is even more exclusive due to their considerably higher fees and more demanding selection procedures. Upper-class children are predominant there. It was taken for granted that Prince Charles' sons would be educated at Eton, just as it is a matter of course for the children of influential bankers or industrialists, senior judges, and diplomats. The father of every third pupil at Eton was himself an Etonian (Adonis and Pollard 1997: 25, 39).

This process of social selection continues, if not to the same extent as at the best public schools, at the two elite universities Oxford and Cambridge. There is one principal reason for this. The percentage of young public school graduates who go on to attend one of these two universities is far higher than the average for graduates of other schools. If one in ten graduates of the top three state schools is admitted to Cambridge, the figure for Westminster graduates is one in three. Six percent of first-year students at Cambridge are recruited from only ten public schools. The picture at Oxford is similar. Today, as in the past few decades, every other Oxford student has attended a public school (Adonis and Pollard 1997: 24, 55–6).

This success is the result first and foremost of a strict selection of applicants and the better quality of education at public schools, for Oxford and Cambridge have particularly stringent entrance requirements. Not only do they require applicants to take a difficult entrance examination, as a rule only candidates with very good grades are even admitted to the examination. In 1980, for example, 83 percent of the new students at Cambridge and 72 percent of those at Oxford had earned very good grades, whereas the corresponding figure for other universities was only 27 percent (Adonis and Pollard 1997: 58). The most renowned public schools, such as Eton, St Paul's, and Westminster, which outperform not only state-run schools but also most of the other public schools (the latter by 40 percent on average) in terms of final grades, are consequently particularly well represented among students there. This discrepancy is primarily the result of the higher quality of education at public schools, which have far smaller classes, generally better-paid and more carefully selected teachers, better equipment, and far more space for a large variety of sports and leisure activities. Better school performance is then complemented by the traditionally close connections between the renowned public schools and the two top universities. Similarities in habitus can be seen among the faculties of these schools and universities (a high percentage of them are recruited from former pupils and students) as well as between staff/faculty and graduates or applicants.

A degree from Oxford or Cambridge and, to an even greater extent, a diploma from one of the famous public schools opens doors to society's top positions. For example, 72 percent of the "chairmen" of the 200 largest British companies completed schooling at one of the 20 most distinguished public schools, which produce a total of only 2,500 graduates a year, and more than 40 went on to get a degree from Oxford or Cambridge. A further 20 or more others also obtained degrees from Oxford or Cambridge. This weighting in favor of the elite educational institutions is even more marked when we look at the country's 100 largest corporations. More than three-quarters of their chairmen have attended one of the 27 most reputable public schools, 11 of them Eton and a further 14 one of the other eight Clarendon schools. Furthermore, almost one in two has a degree from Oxford or Cambridge. If we then include the 12 chairmen who, after graduating from a public school (mostly Eton), trained as officers in the Queen's Guard, a traditional stronghold of the upper class, or trained as accountants at the equally highly regarded Institute of Chartered Accountants, we cannot fail to note that roughly two-thirds enjoyed a decidedly elite education. The financial sector, by far the most important and respectable sector of the economy, stands out in this respect. Almost 90 percent of the country's 25 leading banks and insurance companies are headed by former public school students, nearly a third of them Etonians and almost two-thirds Oxbridge graduates (Bauer and Bertin-Mourot 1996: 101–4; Hartmann 2001a: 165–6).

As far as heads of government are concerned, the situation is much the same as in France. Only three of 12 prime ministers since 1945 have not studied at Oxford or Cambridge, among them Churchill, who chose a career as an officer instead. John Major, another of those without any such exclusive education, headed a Cabinet of 23, 18 of whom were Oxbridge graduates. This was also the case for 12 of his 18 permanent secretaries. In post-war Conservative cabinets the percentage of Oxbridge graduates among members of the government always ranged between 70 and 80 percent. Labour governments did not cross the 50 percent mark until after 1970, a figure which Tony Blair's present cabinet – with its average of 40 percent – has been unable to hold. On the other hand, the percentage among the permanent secretaries has remained much the same since 1945. Under for the most part Conservative governments in power between 1945 and 1964, the average figure was 61 percent; it then rose to as high as 69 percent under the predominantly Labour governments between 1965 and 1979, falling back to only 56 percent under Margaret Thatcher, only to rise again to two-thirds under John Major (Adonis and Pollard 1997: 47–8, 59; Barberis 1996: 99; Mougel 1990: 86–7).

More than three-quarters of John Major's cabinet ministers had attended a public school. In prior Conservative post-war governments the figure had always been more than four-fifths, while the corresponding figures for Labour governments ranged only between one-fifth and one-third. This reflects the recruitment policies of the leading public schools, which must be termed exclusive even in comparison with Oxford and Cambridge. Since 1945 the percentage of permanent secretaries who attended public schools has remained constant at over 60 percent – regardless of the party in power – reaching a maximum of 66 percent for the years 1979 to 1994. Here, the percentage accounted for by the best-known public schools ranges between 20 and 28. Between one in five and one in seven permanent secretaries attended one of the "Clarendon Nine." Under Major almost one in four had attended Eton. If the statistics are extended to include the top people in the senior civil service, the picture remains much the same. In 1994, of the 143 members of the two highest levels, Grade 1 (permanent secretary) and Grade 2 (deputy secretary), over 60 percent were Oxford or Cambridge graduates, while the corresponding percentage for the 447 Grade 3 civil servants (under-secretary) was still as high as 45 percent. Nearly 50 percent of the country's 590 top civil servants had attended a public school. The army and the judiciary present a similar picture. At the end of the 1990s 55 percent of the country's 45 most senior judges had attended a public school, and just under 62 percent had graduated from Oxford or Cambridge. Of the new senior judges appointed by Blair's government since 1997, 79 percent had attended a public school, almost a quarter Eton alone, and 73 percent were Oxford or Cambridge graduates. In 1987 nearly two-thirds of the 214 members of the admiralty and the general staff had attended public schools. One in four army generals had been to Eton. They did not, however, tend to go on to study at Oxbridge – only one in six did so – most of them instead opting for immediate officer training at Sandhurst. Little has changed since then. Of 180 newly trained officers who left Sandhurst in 1995, 120, or exactly two-thirds, had attended public school, and one-quarter had been to one of the top 15 public schools (Adonis and Pollard 1997: 48, 125; Barberis 1996: 105; Dargie and Locke 1999: 192; Mougel 1990: 86–7, 343).

In view of this preponderance of the exclusive public schools and the two elite universities, it is not surprising to note that the social recruitment of British elites is similar to that of their French counterparts. Every other chairman of the country's 100 largest companies is from the upper class; in the financial sector the proportion is as high as three in four; a further third are recruited from the remaining upper middle classes (Hartmann 1997: 9–10; 2001a: 167–8; 2002: 159). There is, then, no appreciable difference between Britain and France in this regard. Politics and administration, on the other hand, do not present such a uniform picture. By the mid-1960s the predominance of upper-class, Conservative prime ministers à la Churchill and Macmillan had come to and end. Of the six subsequent prime ministers, none came from the upper class; indeed, one-third each were recruited from the upper middle class, the middle classes, or more humble origins. This social opening of the post of prime minister is reflected only in part in certain, predominantly Conservative, cabinets. In the period between 1979 and 1987, about two-thirds of Margaret Thatcher's cabinet members came from the upper class, a decline of no more than roughly 10 percent compared with earlier Tory governments. The only big loser was the nobility; its share declined from one-third to just below one-tenth. These changes have generally affected the permanent secretaries to a far lesser degree. The majority of them continue to be recruited from upper middle-class backgrounds (Barberis 1996: 74; Mougel 1990: 86–7).

Although their influence is uncontested, the Oxford and Cambridge old boy networks do not have the same quality as the networks of the Polytechniciens or the Enarques. The reason for this is the far higher number of students at Oxford and Cambridge and the fact that these two universities are not as socially exclusive as their French counterparts. The old-boy networks of the famous public schools, however, are comparable in almost every respect. This goes in particular for former Etonians. Their network is generally regarded as the most successful in the whole of Britain. It includes the "heads" of 35 of the country's 200 wealthiest families (Scott 1991: 114). All in all, the alumni associations of the renowned public schools, and of Oxford and Cambridge, operate in ways quite similar to the networks of former Grandes écoles graduates, although the former are not quite as tightly and efficiently organized as the latter.

5.3 The US: St Grottlesex and the Ivy League

At first sight the education system for the US elite resembles the British system in many points. Here, too, there are exclusive private schools – mostly situated on the east coast; these include institutions like Phillips Exeter[5] or Groton, which are comparable to the British public schools, and elite universities such as Harvard, Yale, or Princeton. However, if we look more closely, we note two crucial differences, despite the similarities. First, compared with their British counterparts, the American private schools play no more than a subordinate role in the selection process. Unlike Eton, for example, these schools do not ensure direct access to society's top positions but represent a preliminary stage on the path toward the elite universities crucial to a good career. These universities in turn – and this is the second major difference – are privately owned and run. The most distinguished US state university, Berkeley, reaches at best place 20 in the rankings.

A brief glance at the exclusive private schools on the east coast, often referred to as St Grottlesex, an amalgamation of the names of three famous schools, St Paul's, Groton, and Middlesex, immediately reveals parallels to the well-known British public schools. Schools such as Phillips Exeter Academy, Taft School, or St Paul's ensure a high degree of social exclusiveness by virtue of their tuition fees, which amount to about $25,000, and overall fees (including room and board) totaling a good $33,000. Despite the fact that one in three students receives financial support in the form of a scholarship, more than 80 percent of their students come from the top fifth of society. Almost half the families who send their children to private boarding schools have incomes four times the national average, and a further 20 percent have incomes three to four times this average (Cookson and Persell 1985: 58). For these extremely high fees the schools offer an excellent education that paves the way to the elite universities. Not only are they better equipped and staffed, their student–teacher ratios – roughly five students per teacher (instead of the usual 15 in state schools) – are far better. On the annual scholastic aptitude tests taken throughout the country, students of these private schools reach scores of between 650 and 700 in the two categories verbal and math (on a scale from 200 to 800 points), results which are far above the average score of 500 points.

Their prospects of being accepted by one of the elite universities are accordingly good. True, in contrast to earlier times, when three-quarters of Phillips Exeter's graduates went on to study at Harvard, at present "only" about one-sixth do so. However, if the admission figures for Phillips Exeter and Phillips Andover are added together, they account for 90 of a total of roughly 1,600 admissions (Levy 1990: 56–7). These two schools alone, which produce no more than 600 to 700 of a total of over two million high school graduates a year, account for over 5 percent of first-year students at Harvard. On the whole, when it comes to getting admitted to one of the top universities, graduates of the famed private schools – with their admission rates of 38 to 40 percent – do almost as well as the offspring of alumni from these universities, who have a rate of 40 to 42 percent. In other words, these two groups lie way ahead of other applicants, whose chances of admission are no higher than 10 to 20 percent, depending on the university in question.[6]

As might to be expected in the light of these figures, the social composition of the student bodies of the US' renowned elite universities shows signs of extreme selectivity. This is essentially in line with the situation at the country's exclusive private schools. In both cases four-fifths of students come from the top 20 percent of US society, while the lower half of the population is hardly represented at all (Hartmann 2005). Three factors are responsible for this. First, children from the upper classes and strata of society achieve better results on aptitude tests. From their early years on, their family backgrounds have provided them with more favorable conditions for intellectual development, and they enjoy better schooling, be it because of their place of residence or because of their parents' financial potential, which permits them to send their children to expensive private schools.

If students from exclusive private schools are left out of consideration, however, the performance figures for children from families belonging to the upper 10 percent of income earners have an edge of no more than 10 percent, despite all the advantages these children enjoy. For this reason, two other points must be regarded as more important for social selection. First, the costs of studying at an elite university are extremely high. They amount to over $40,000 annually for an undergraduate studying for a bachelor's degree and to over $50,000 per year for all postgraduate courses of study. These sums are the equivalent of average US family incomes. The comprehensive financial support programs provided by these universities can do no more than slightly alleviate the social selection effect which inevitably results. Of the full-time undergraduate students at private universities with low or average family incomes, almost 90 percent receive financial support; but for almost three-quarters of all recipients this support consists, to a greater or lesser extent, of loans. Although the two most important types of low-interest loan, the government-supported "Federal Perkins Loan" and "Federal Stafford Loan" programs, have relatively moderate interest rates, undergraduates with a high loan ratio can end up with debts totaling about $60,000 by the end of their undergraduate studies, and over $100,000 if they go on to study for a master's degree, PhD, or a professional degree.

An average student, including all those students who attend state universities or colleges with considerably lower fees of, for example, only $2,000 to $3,000, today incurs a debt of around $30,000. This figure has more than doubled over the past seven years. This debt situation is bound to deteriorate even further due to increases in university fees (over 50 percent in the last ten years), which are far outpacing income growth. There is reason to assume that this debt situation will have an above-average effect on graduates from top universities (Hartmann 2005). Even though government pays the interest on a large proportion of such debts, up to a maximum of about $40,000 (undergraduate) or $100,000 (graduate/professional), all those who have to finance a large part of their studies in this way are still faced with an enormous financial burden. This of course acts as a deterrent to potential applicants from the working class or the broad middle classes – to a far greater extent than for children of wealthy families.

The admissions committees responsible for final decisions on admission are the second crucial hurdle as far as social selection is concerned. The elite universities not only explicitly seek applicants with the best test results, they are also interested in personalities who might prove to be a "gain" for the university. In other words, a candidate's personality is, ultimately, the decisive factor. "Leadership," for instance, is a central criterion for the director of Harvard's Admission Committee (*Business Week*, 23 August 2000). The vice-president of the University of Denver formulates his central criterion for selection interviews in a way quite similar to that outlined by the member of the ENA commission quoted above. For him, too, the main consideration is "whether you would want this person as a classmate or roommate" (*The Boston Globe*, 13 January 2004). As Feldman (1988) points out plainly in her study on the admission procedures at Harvard, such standards clearly favor the offspring of the "better circles." Candidates from private schools, for example, do considerably better than other candidates as far as personality assessment is concerned; however, when the admissions committee appraises the intellectual aptitude of applicants, it finds no differences whatever.

The reasons for this edge are at the same time "objective" and "subjective," that is, the reasons must be sought in the committee's point of view. Viewed objectively, children who have attended a private school, and in particular a renowned private school, have enjoyed a wide spectrum of measures designed to shape and broaden their personality. But one factor equally as important, indeed possibly even more important, is that applicants and commission members often concur on certain assessment criteria, e.g. behavior patterns. In their evaluation of a candidate's personality, the commission members – and this is the subjective aspect of the selection process – favor (consciously or unconsciously) attitudes and behaviors that are by and large the same as their own.[7] In view of the fact that commission members are highly qualified and come from the upper strata of society, this applies above all for candidates from renowned private schools, the "better circles" of society. There are now even special coaches who prepare candidates specifically for the entrance examinations of the elite universities, for fees of up to $33,000. They give tips, edit application documents, conduct practice interviews, etc. Just a one-day visit to the campus at Harvard or Yale can cost up to $4,000. Such sums of money are beyond the means of ordinary families. So the children of the "upper ten thousand" not only profit in a general way from the personality elements they owe to their social background, they are also able to build systematically on these advantages thanks to the financial means available to their families.

Two additional mechanisms serve to further bolster the preferential treatment accorded to these applicants. First, there are close contacts between the well-known private schools and the famous private universities. These are systematically cultivated, particularly as far as the rapport between the principals of the schools and the university admissions committees are concerned. Second, the private universities are largely dependent on donations from wealthy alumni or the companies in which they are active. This is the reason why the children of alumni are given preferential treatment in the form of quotas – this provides universities access to financial resources. These students are spoken of frankly as "'lineage' types – 'candidates who probably couldn't be admitted without the extra plus of being a Harvard son'" (Feldman 1988: 95).

In recent years the elite universities have even begun to adopt the practice of scouting for students who would have no chance of admission on the grounds of their performance but who have very wealthy parents, even though they may not be alumni of the university concerned. The goal is to win over their families. At Duke University, traditionally one of the top 20 US universities, indeed at present among the top ten, 500 such candidates are identified annually, 40 of whom are admitted directly and almost 100 more of whom are accepted after lengthy discussions. Although only a good two-thirds of them actually register, they still account for 3 to 5 percent of new students. In this way the universities aim to increase the number of fully paying students and at the same time to boost the number of potential donors – with a view to compensating at least in part for losses sustained in the recent the stock market crash. In her study Feldman comes to the conclusion that the current selection system has, generally speaking, the same social effect as auctioning off university places to the highest bidder. If, on the other hand, university places were allocated purely on the basis of chance or achievement, the number of students who have alumni parents or have graduated from a well-known private school would be almost halved (Feldman 1988: 176–7). All in all, it can be said that the admissions procedures at the distinguished elite universities very effectively ensure that the offspring of society's top 20 percent remain largely among themselves.

Despite the unquestionable importance of exclusive educational institutions (particularly universities) in the US, their influence is not as great as it is in the UK or France; this is due to the size of the country and to its federal structure. Graduates from the famous elite universities are, admittedly, completely disproportionately represented in the top levels of business and politics, but the weight they carry cannot be compared with that of the Enarques or Etonians. This is evident in the business sector, the area where they are best represented. At the beginning of the 1980s, 50 percent of the top managers of the 265 largest American corporations had studied at one of only 12 top universities, a rate comparable to that in Britain or France. But if we reduce this figure to the top 100 corporations, the rise in this percentage that might be expected fails to materialize. "Only" four in ten CEOs of these companies were alumni of the 13 top universities,[8] although one in four had attended one of only four of these universities, and 12 were Harvard graduates (Dye 1995: 171; Hartmann 2001a: 167).[9] As remarkable as this concentration on a limited number of elite universities, and in particular on Harvard, may be, the situation is in no way comparable with the situation at the ENA or École Polytechnique in France or Oxford and Cambridge in the UK.

In politics the picture is similar. Graduates from the elite universities are heavily represented, but they do not have the same weight as Enarques or Oxbridge alumni. Four of the 12 US presidents since 1945 studied at Yale, but "only" one in two of the rest studied at one of the other top 20 universities. Besides, the procession of Yale graduates began only in 1989 with the inauguration of George Bush. He, like his two successors, Bill Clinton and George W. Bush, is a Yale graduate. The same, incidentally, is true of John Kerry, Bush's contender for the presidency in the 2004 elections. Al Gore, who lost to Bush in the last US presidential election, attended Harvard. Furthermore, two key ministries, the Department of Defense and the Department of Justice, are headed by Yale and Harvard alumni.

The steep increase in the influence of Yale and Harvard graduates goes hand in hand with a marked increase in the direct political influence of the traditional upper class. Both Bush senior and Bush junior and Al Gore come from "big" upper-class families, and all three attended one of the famous east coast private schools. The picture is rounded off by John Kerry, another child of the east coast upper class, former student of an exclusive private school, and married to the heiress to the Heinz Ketchup empire. While John F. Kennedy had been the only one of the other eight post-war US presidents to come from the upper class, and thus to have attended a highly exclusive private school before going on to Harvard, the situation has changed fundamentally in the past 15 years. The "ordinary people" whose offspring provided the majority of presidents up to the end of the 1980s have lost considerable ground. The sons of the upper class, on the other hand, are better represented now than they have been for decades. This reflects overall shifts in power within American society. Due to a lack of precise data it is not possible to give an accurate picture of the situation in the business sector, where, up to the 1980s, between a third and a half of top managers were recruited from the upper class (Dye 1995: 175; Hartmann 1996: 172). It may, however, be assumed that the percentage has increased here, too.[10] Generally speaking, though, the social recruitment of the US business elite is probably not as selective as it is in the case of their French and British counterparts.

5.4 Japan: the Todai connection

In no other industrialized nation does a single educational institution play such a large role in accessing key leadership positions as the Todai, the Japanese state Imperial University of Tokyo. In this respect it even outdoes the ENA, which, after all, has a more or less equal rival in the École Polytechnique. Japanese families, then, who wish to give their children the opportunity to reach top positions in business, politics, or administration have just one goal: their children must pass the entrance examination to the Todai, or at least to one of Japan's other top four universities (the state Kyodai University, the public Hitotsubashi University, or the private universities of Keio and Waseda).

The Japanese education system is extraordinarily hierarchical. There are nation-wide rankings for every type of school, college, or university which define the exact position of each individual institution. The high road to the Todai, then, begins practically with attendance at the "right" kindergarten. The truly vital stage, however, is admission to one of the country's best secondary preparatory schools, for while only 0.2 per mill of all secondary school graduates are able to study at the Todai, up to 50 percent of graduates from these top schools are admitted. These schools are thus in great demand. All of Japan's leading secondary preparatory schools are private institutions which, in addition to admission fees of up to several thousand euro, charge roughly equally high annual fees. Then there are additional fees for more or less obligatory schools that provide extra tuition, the so-called *jukus*. These jukus are attended by nearly all secondary preparatory school students (as well as by the majority of high school students), because only these schools impart the full range of knowledge required for the entrance examinations to the top universities (or distinguished secondary preparatory schools).[11] For example, the official curriculum of the preparatory schools teaches students only two-thirds of the vocabulary they need to pass the English test at Todai or Waseda. In other words, to acquire the knowledge required, students must have attended a juku. The good jukus cost up to several thousand euro a year, in addition to regular school fees.

School costs can easily amount to as much as €10,000 per year. Accordingly, the financial aspect plays a role that should not be underestimated, although it does not have the same weight as in the UK or the US. In fact, the Japanese selection procedure, with its rigid entrance examinations, is, on the whole, not unlike the French system. This means that the social selection of students is not as rigid as it is at the UK's renowned public schools or the US's highly regarded east coast private schools. Still, it is a real factor. At one of the most famous preparatory schools in Japan, the Nada in Kobe, as early as the mid-1970s, for example, 60 percent of students came from university-educated families. Yet less than 5 percent of men from this parental generation had attended a university. So it is not surprising that the fathers of one in eight pupils were either doctors or professors and that the fathers of one in seven were senior business executives (Rohlen 1983: 130–2).

This university selection process has since continued at a more rigorous level (again, there are similarities with France). Nearly all students at the Todai come from the top 10 percent of Japanese society (Cutts 1997: 231). The decisive factor here is not tuition fees, which are in fact a good deal lower than those of the well-known preparatory schools, but rigorous university entrance examinations. The top Japanese universities employ mechanisms similar to those used by the ENA or the École Polytechnique to ensure that most applicants from the broad population are excluded. This also applies for the two most distinguished private elite universities, Keio and Waseda. With fees ranging from €7,000 to €10,000 per year (depending on course of study) and entrance fees of about €2,000, they are considerably more expensive than the two top state universities, Todai and Kyodai; nonetheless, cost is not the decisive factor for social selection.

The parallels with the renowned Grandes écoles can also be seen in the way that top positions are allocated in Japanese society. The Todai, with its 15,000 or more undergraduates, a proportion of just 5 per mill of all Japanese students, is dominant in business, politics, and administration to an extent paralleled only by the ENA. Of the 25 Japanese prime ministers since 1945, ten studied there, all of them at the law faculty, a department attended by no more than a good tenth of all Todai students. In Prime Minister Koizumi's current cabinet, six of a total of 18 members are Todai alumni. Four of them, including the heads of three of the key ministries (Finance, Justice and Economic Affairs, and Trade and Industry) studied at the Todai law faculty. In the 1990s one-quarter of all members of parliament belonging to the LPD (the party which has been in power without interruption since the Second World War) had studied at the Todai. If the figures for the opposition are included, this figure declines, but it still reaches a remarkable 20 percent.

The influence of Todai graduates is far more pronounced at the top echelons of state bureaucracy than it is in politics. Under Prime Minister Miyazawa (1991–1993) 18 of 20 ministerial undersecretaries were graduates of this one university. This is typical of government administration. The first step is the entrance examination for Career Track I, which has to be passed if a candidate wishes to attain a leadership position. Of over 30,000 applicants, fewer than 2,000 pass the test, and only about half of these are actually hired. More than 30 percent of successful candidates, and almost 40 percent of those subsequently hired, had studied at the Todai. Among the candidates who take the so-called "fast track" there is an even larger proportion of Todai alumni. This fast-track system opens the door to the top positions in the most important ministries and is open to about 300 persons per year, about 70 of these positions being in the two most important ministries, the Ministry of Finance (MoF) and the Ministry for International Trade and Industry (MITI). Roughly two-thirds of these persons are Todai graduates, and over three-quarters of those hired by MoF and MITI are also recruited among Todai alumni, the large majority from one faculty, namely law, with its 400 to 500 graduates per year. Of the 14 judges at Japan's Supreme Court, eight are law faculty graduates. The majority of teaching staff at the Todai are also Todai alumni (Cutts 1997: 67).

The top positions not filled by Todai graduates are usually given to applicants from one of the other four renowned elite universities. Of the remaining 13 prime ministers, five attended Waseda University, two Keio, one Kyodai, and one Hitotsubashi. Only six of a total of 25 prime ministers had not graduated from one of these elite institutions. Five ministers in the present cabinet studied at Keio (including Prime Minister Koizumi), two at Hitotsubashi, and one at Waseda. Only four of 18 cabinet members (all in less prestigious departments such as Health, Youth, or Environment) attended other universities. In the mid-1990s, graduates of Waseda, Keio, Kyodai, and Hitotsubashi Universities accounted for a further 30 percent of the LDP members of parliament, and the same was the case for 20 percent of successful applicants for Career Track I (Cutts 1997: 4–5, 178–9; Kerbo and McKinstry 1995: 140; Rothacher 1993: 71, 128–30). A further three of the country's 14 highest-ranking judges also studied at Keio.

The picture in the business sector is a similar one. In the mid-1980s almost 23 percent of presidents of companies listed on the Tokyo Stock Exchange were graduates of Todai, and a further 28 percent had graduated from the other four top universities. This concentration on the leading elite universities is even more conspicuous in the 100 largest Japanese companies. Forty of their presidents came from Todai and a further 22 from the other four leading universities. The picture changes very little when other top executives are included. In the Mitsubishi Group, the largest of the Japanese consolidated companies (*keiretsu*), one in three company directors is a Todai graduate, while a further third come from the other four top universities (Cutts 1997: 183; Hartmann 2002: 154; Ishida 1993: 153). Two-thirds of the business elite attended one of the five most famous universities, over one-third Todai, and at Todai most of them studied law. With its 400 to 500 graduates per annum – that is, no more than 0.5 per mill of all university graduates and only 0.2 per mill of one cohort – this faculty accounts for about one in three top managers, two in three top ministerial officials, and four in ten prime ministers. Worldwide, the ENA is the only other institution that can boast of similar results.

The high level of social selectivity in Japan's elite educational institutions and their extraordinary importance in the filling of top positions are good reasons to assume that recruitment to Japanese social elites is likewise exclusive in nature. Although detailed information is only available for the political sphere, it is highly likely that this assumption is, on the whole, realistic; in Japan even the political elite, which in most other countries is quite open to various social strata, is dominated to a surprisingly high degree by something very much like family dynasties. One hundred and thirty of the 500 or more representatives in the lower house of the Japanese parliament come from families of former members of parliament, some of them from the third generation. The figure for the parliamentary faction of the LDP is over one-third, and reaches a level of 41 percent in the highest positions (Kerbo and McKinstry 1995: 107; Rothacher 1993: 50). The corresponding figures for post-war-era prime ministers is close to two-thirds, that is, 15 of 23. The fathers of three of the six last prime ministers also held important political posts, while two of their fathers were major entrepreneurs (one of them also a provincial governor). The current prime minister, Junichiro Koizumi, is a typical example. Although he is generally considered a reformer and opponent of the party establishment, he does actually come from an old and very influential family of politicians. His father was defense minister and his grandfather minister of postal services. The process of recruitment to the Japanese leadership elite does not, then, appear to differ appreciably from that in France, the UK, or the US. In all these countries it is people from upper or upper middle-class backgrounds who play the predominant roles.

5.5 Germany: PhDs and upper middle-class habitus

Germany differs from the other four countries under consideration here in that as yet it has no elite educational institutions, either at the school or the university level. The only German qualification which is in any way comparable to the exclusive degrees awarded by the elite institutions in these countries is the doctorate. The number of German students earning a doctorate, the highest German academic title,[12] ranged between 5,000 and 10,000 in the 1950s and 1960s, a figure considerably higher than the numbers of students graduating from the elite institutions in France, the UK, or Japan. However, if we look only at graduates in the three disciplines in demand for the vast majority of top positions, the picture is quite different. During the period in question the number of PhDs awarded in the fields of engineering, law, and economics ranged between 1,300 and 2,000, qualitative dimensions wholly comparable to the situation at the elite educational institutions of France, the UK, Japan and, perhaps above all, the US. This picture changed perceptibly only when the education sector began to expand. Today, over 22,000 students are awarded PhDs each year, and this development has also affected the three disciplines mentioned above, which now account for some 4,500 doctorates per annum (Hartmann 2002: 198).

The power of social selection once embodied in a PhD has thus diminished accordingly. Up to the 1970s more than 60 percent of PhD holders in engineering, law, and economics came from the upper middle-class backgrounds, but this figure is now likely to have declined to less than 50 percent.[13] However, even at the rate of 60 percent that was normal in the past, a doctoral degree from a German university is nowhere near as socially exclusive as degrees from the ENA, the École Polytechnique, Oxbridge, Harvard, Yale, or the Todai. What, even back then, distinguished a German doctorate fundamentally from diplomas from these elite institutions was the lower level of social prestige it bestowed – despite the fact that its holder was entitled to a good measure of respect – as well as the lack of that certain sense of togetherness felt by graduates of these other institutions. Two factors were (and still are today) responsible for this comparative lack of social prestige: first, the fact that the aim of the doctorate, as opposed to a diploma from a famous public school or Grande école, is not to enhance the holder's elite consciousness or status; indeed the primary aim was and is acquisition of academic knowledge. The second factor involved is the far higher overall number of PhDs awarded – that is, if we include all other disciplines in the figures. This lack of an esprit de corps results from the fact that in Germany earning a PhD is a highly individualized process as well as from the fact that to date there is no hierarchical ranking of German universities, and thus where one has studied for a doctorate is a matter of relative indifference.

Even so, doctorates were and still are extremely common among members of German social elites. Over 50 percent of the chairmen of the executive and supervisory boards of the 100 largest German companies, every other high-ranking civil servant and judge, and naturally all professors, have a PhD. With the exception of the latter, 90 percent of these PhDs are in the fields of engineering, law, or economics. In politics, though, a PhD is as good as irrelevant. In other words, with the exception of politics, the social

selectivity implied by the PhD may indeed be seen as having a certain pre-
selection function to the benefit of the offspring of the upper middle class.
This, however, is not sufficient to explain why the social selection of top
German executives turns out to be just as exclusive as it is in the case of
their French or British counterparts. The reason for the fact that almost half
of all executive chairmen (*Vorstandsvorsitzende*) in the 100 largest German
companies come from the upper classes and a further third are recruited
from the upper middle classes[14] (Hartmann 2000: 248), whereas only one of
eight German chancellors grew up in a middle-class milieu, must thus be
sought elsewhere.

A look at the educational and professional careers of all those awarded a
doctorate in engineering, law, or economics in the years 1955, 1965, 1975,
and 1985 – a total of some 6,500 persons (Hartmann 2002) – brings us
closer to an answer. The conditions required for advancement into the elite,
both in the broad[15] and in the narrow sense, varies (to a greater or lesser
degree) from sector to sector. At first sight a middle-class background
appears to be an uncontested advantage only in the business sector. Of those
PhD holders whose fathers were workers, farmers, lower-grade white-collar
workers or civil servants, or small self-employed persons, slightly less than
one in ten was promoted to the top management level of a large enterprise
in the course of his or her professional career. By comparison, more than one
in eight of those with an upper middle-class background and almost one in
five of those with an upper-class background managed to secure a position of
this kind. If we differentiate further, we find that people from a working-
class background have the worst chances, while the sons of major entrepreneurs have the best chances. The latter are three times as successful as the
former. People from upper- and upper middle-class backgrounds are not so
dominant in other sectors. In fact, in academic fields PhD holders from the
broader population prove more successful than this group.

However, we find a striking change in the picture when we restrict our
view to the elite in the narrow sense of the term. Here, in the top echelons of
the largest 400 German corporations, the major business associations, and
the federal courts, the sons of the upper-middle and particularly of the upper
classes clearly play a dominant role. On the path to the boardrooms of the
major German corporations the sons of the upper-middle classes are twice as
successful as the sons of the population at large, and the sons of the upper
classes are even more than three times as successful as the rest of the population. Indeed, the children of executives achieve such positions ten times
and the children of top executives 17 times more often than persons from a
working-class background. The chances of a top executive with an upper-
class background also becoming a leading figure in an industrial association
are three times higher than for a PhD holder from the population at large.
The picture is similar in the top echelons of the judiciary. While the judiciary elite, in the wider sense of the term, recruits nearly half of its PhD
holders from the broad population, the corresponding figure declines to only

one-third when it comes to federal judges, and no more than one in eight judges at Germany's two second highest federal courts[16] (after the constitutional court), namely the Federal Supreme Court of Justice and the Federal Administrative Court. PhD holders with an upper-class background account for more than a quarter of all federal judges and even one-third of the judges active at the two above-named high federal courts. Of all jurists from an upper-class background who hold a doctorate, almost one in three holds a position as a federal judge. In other words, the more important and influential a position is, the lower the chances are that a person from the broad population will be recruited for it. The reverse is the case when we look at the sons of the upper-middle and, above all, the upper classes. They are particularly well represented among the elite in the narrow sense of the term.

The university record of children from an upper- or middle-class background is not sufficient to explain their far better career prospects among the elite in the narrow sense as well as in business in general. While it is true that on average upper middle-class PhD holders complete their studies one semester earlier than their counterparts from the rest of the population, and almost twice as many of them have also studied abroad, and that this certainly improves their career prospects in large corporations, this fact in no way diminishes the important role played by social origin. This is verified beyond doubt by calculations which address all of the factors involved[17] and the ways in which they interrelate. Parental background has a very direct influence on access to the German elite.

If we take a look, first, at the business sector, which is of key importance in this respect – more than two-thirds of PhD holders belonging to the elite are active in this sector – we find that, beyond doubt, the major reason for the far higher success rate noted for children of the upper-middle classes is their class-specific habitus. Anyone aspiring to a position in board rooms and the top management of large corporations must have, more than anything else, one particular feature: his habitus must resemble that of the persons already in these positions. Since decisions bearing on top positions in large corporations are made by a very small circle of people, and since the procedure involved is not particularly formalized, the key factor here is similarity with the so-called "decision-makers," i.e. to seem to be "cut from the same cloth." These decisions are based far less on rational criteria than is generally assumed.

The crucial significance of the "right chemistry" or "feel" is bound up largely with the need to have people in one's entourage whom one feels one can trust. As one top executive put it in an interview, the boardroom must, as a rule, be seen as a "community of fate," as a group that either succeeds or fails together. The major factor that decides on whether or not a person is regarded as trustworthy, and thus as acceptable as a boardroom colleague, is, ultimately, habitus.

There are four central personality characteristics that serve to define the habitus desired in the top echelons of large German corporations.

A candidate must demonstrate intimate knowledge of the required codes of dress and etiquette; this, from the point of view of the decision-maker, shows whether the candidate knows and is prepared to embrace the written and, above all, the unwritten rules and laws of the top echelons of the business sector. Here a good and broad-based general education is regarded as a clear and desirable indicator of the celebrated ability "to think outside of the box" that is considered vital to such positions.[18] An entrepreneurial attitude (including the optimistic outlook on life that top executives believe this necessarily implies) is considered imperative, because without it "visions" are thought not to be possible. Supreme self-assurance in appearance and manner is considered, in the eyes of the decision-makers, the most important element that distinguishes persons suitable for management positions of this caliber.

As cogent as these explanations may seem to be, the real issue is quite a different one. In describing these traits, decision-makers are in fact only describing the man they see in themselves. Their belief in themselves as the right man in the right place leads top executives to seek out others with the same or similar characteristics. This, however, means, in the end, that they show a clear preference for people who, like themselves, come from the upper or upper middle classes. These people demonstrate the same self-assurance that is both desired and expected. It is, of course, easiest for those who have grown up in such a milieu to behave as if they had always been at home in a boardroom environment. People on the way up the social ladder are nearly always lacking in the required, or at least desired, measure of ease of manner and behavior and thus not in a position or prepared, when occasion calls, to skillfully question, or, should the situation arise, simply break the official canon and the ruling codes. This level of self-assuredness, which involves a playful handling of the rules in force, constitutes the central difference between those who belong and those who would only like to belong.

The far better career prospects enjoyed in other areas of society by PhD holders from the broader strata of the populace indicate that both the habitus requirements and selection mechanisms in these areas differ to a greater or lesser degree from those in the business sector. This is a simple fact. A career in politics continues to be based on the principle of the "hard slog." What this means is that anyone aspiring to a seat in the Bundestag or a leadership position in a state ministry has to launch his or her career at a low level in a local party organization.[19] "A steady and uninterrupted career within a party, usually starting out with local party leadership positions, [is] a prerequisite nearly indispensable for attaining national leadership positions" (Herzog 1990: 36). The comparatively democratic selection processes in Germany's major popular parties ensure that the relatively broad social diversity of the party base has an influence on candidate selection that should not be underestimated. Another important point is that politicians who aspire to success must at least have a certain affinity to their voter clientele. All this works to the benefit of potential candidates whose habitus does not deviate too sharply from what is expected by the much-invoked grass-roots. Even so, the consequence of the erosion of the major popular parties has been that the number of politicians of upper middle-class origins has grown appreciably. To cite an instance, Roland Koch and Friedrich März, two of the three most influential politicians of the CDU, and Guido Wester-welle, chairman of the FDP, all come from established lawyer families. What is more, two daughters of prominent former state prime ministers hold positions in two state cabinets, the daughter of Franz Josef Strauss in Bavaria and the daughter of Ernst Albrecht in Lower Saxony.

Looking at the judiciary as opposed to the business sector, it may be said that there are three principle factors that serve to improve the career opportunities of PhD holders from the working class and the broad middle classes, namely highly formalized hiring procedures, a typically civil-service habitus, and the influence of politics on the personnel decisions taken at higher levels. The situation is similar in academia. Before a person is appointed professor, he or she has to traverse several strongly formalized stages of an appointment procedure. Also, it is important not to underesti-mate nonuniversity political influences. These two factors serve to rule out any simple "cooptation" by a limited number of decision-makers, the usual practice in business. Furthermore, the characteristic academic habitus of "knowledge orientation" and "avid cultural interest" is far more amenable to young people from the broad strata of the population than the image of the "supremely self-assured man of action" prevalent in the top echelons of busi-ness. All in all, the rule is that access to elite positions is all the more diffi-cult from a social point of view, the smaller the circle of persons responsible for appointments, and the more informal the selection procedure.

Although there is an obvious correlation between the structure of appointment processes and the social opening of elite positions, this tells only half of the story. The fact that PhD holders from the "normal popu-lation" have far better career prospects in politics, law, and academia than in business cannot be explained solely by the fact that decisions there are made by a larger circle of people following strictly formalized rules, it also has to do with options and priorities.

The chances for people of working class or broad middle-class origin are always better than average when competitors from upper or upper middle-class backgrounds show comparatively little interest in a given position. In fact, the latter are generally drawn to positions promising the greatest power and the highest incomes, i.e. the top echelons of business,[20] while competi-tion in other areas is thus automatically less fierce. This, however, means in effect that lack of interest on the part of "upper-class children" gives rise to career opportunities for PhD holders from other classes of society which are practically nonexistent in large business corporations.

This becomes particularly evident when we compare PhDs awarded in the two years 1965 and 1975. As far as their career prospects are concerned, these two cohorts constitute two extreme poles. Students completing their

PhDs in 1965 encountered extremely favorable conditions, not only because the economic boom in the late 1960s and early 1970s brought excellent career prospects, but also because this was the period in which Germany's civil service and – above all – university system were enlarged, creating new positions and excellent career opportunities for jurists and scholars. The 1975 cohort, on the other hand, found itself faced with particularly difficult circumstances. The economic miracle was over once and for all, and the wave of new appointments at German universities was ebbing out. The number of vacant or newly created top positions was correspondingly low. In Germany the only exception here was, at least to some extent, the judiciary.

The offspring of the upper-middle classes and – above all – of the upper classes responded immediately to the deteriorating situation. They sought to compensate for the tangible decrease in top corporate positions by shifting their focus to other sectors. Upper-class youngsters had no trouble doing so. They were more than able to make up for the slight downward trend of 15 percent in the business sector by taking advantage of marked growth rates at universities (76 percent) and in the judiciary (80 percent). PhD holders from the upper-middle classes were not quite so successful. Not only were their losses in the top echelons of business higher (26 percent), they were also unable to fully compensate for these losses, despite growth rates in the judiciary of 250 percent, because the losses they sustained at the universities (26 percent) were just as high as they were in the business sector.

Yet compared with the losses suffered by PhD holders from the working class and the broad middle classes, these figures are hardly even worth mentioning. The latter groups not only lost one in two top positions in business but also had to contend with a 40 percent decline in university employment. It was only in the judiciary (7 percent growth) that they were able to improve their situation somewhat. Altogether, though, they were faced with losses of almost 40 percent. While more than one-quarter of the 1965 cohort advanced into top positions, the corresponding figures for business and universities being one in eight and one in nine, respectively, only one in seven of the 1975 cohort was this successful. PhD holders with an upper- or upper middle-class background present an entirely different picture. Despite overall losses of around 10 percent, one in five upper middle-class children still managed to achieve excellent careers. Thanks to growth rates of over 10 percent, the corresponding figure for upper-class children was one in three.

A closer look at the judiciary may serve to illustrate the different career prospects open to children from the upper classes on the one hand and children from the rest of the population on the other. From the second half of the 1970s on, jurists were particularly hard hit by the deterioration of career opportunities in business. Not only were they faced with a general reduction in the number of top positions but they also had to contend with the fact that they were being supplanted by business economists, who were increasingly capturing top positions traditionally held by lawyers, first in industry (Hartmann 1990) and later in their classic domain, the financial sector.

Whereas in 1980 almost two-thirds of the board members of the four leading German banks held law degrees, today no more than one-quarter are lawyers (Hartmann 2003: 119–20).[21] In other words, the situation for holders of a PhD in law from the 1975 cohort was fraught with problems. For this reason they set their sights on positions in the judiciary, which then still promised the best career opportunities. Not all were equally successful here. While PhD holders from the working class and the broad middle classes were only able to increase their success rate by something approaching 50 percent, their upper-class contemporaries were twice as successful. Sons of upper middle-class parents, who were more severely affected than upper-class children by developments in the business and university sectors, had success rates four times as high (Hartmann 2002: 103).[22]

All in all, access to German elites has become more increasingly exclusive in social terms over a period in which there has been a broadening of opportunities for PhD study. This holds most particularly for the business sector.[23] But the percentage of elite members from the upper and middle classes active in politics, administration, culture, the mass media, and the military has likewise increased (to a greater or lesser degree) (Schnapp 1997a: 77). The expansion of the education sector has facilitated access only to educational institutions, not to elite positions. Holding over 80 percent of positions in the business sector, and accounting for a share of almost two-thirds of senior administrative officials and judges, the upper and middle classes continue to dominate the picture here.

5.6 Internationalization of elites?

In late March 2001 the president of the French central bank, Jean-Claude Trichet, a former member of the ENA and the Inspection des Finances, predicted, in the German newspaper *Die Zeit*: "In about five years time there will no longer be a single member of the (state-run cadre-training facility) Inspection des Finances, in a top position of a major French bank." In his opinion, globalization of the economy will put an end to this specifically French career model which has ensured that top positions in the country's major financial institutions are filled almost exclusively by former members of this Grand Corps. The end of national elites in favor of transnational elites is being proclaimed not only in France but in Germany and Britain as well. Such predictions have been made repeatedly for the business sector in particular. While the formation of truly influential transnational organizations, and thus transnational elites as well, is progressing at a slow pace in politics, administration, and the judiciary, and while such organizations have repeatedly failed in the face of resistance from national elites over crucial disputes (for example, the UN in the case of the Gulf War or the EU Commission on the issue of national debt), the business sector does not appear to be affected. The growing pace of internationalization appears to be an ideal breeding ground for the internationalization of top positions.

Rosabeth Moss Kanter, former President of the Harvard Business School, chose to give a book she published in 1995 the title *World Class*; Leslie Sklair chose an even more clear-cut title: *The Transnational Capital Class*. In her study, Kanter describes the formation of a new world class of executives and entrepreneurs whose members are not only "cosmopolitan" in orientation but have "very close connections" with one another. These persons, she notes, are the uppermost echelon of a global elite of top managers. Sklair, whose line of argumentation focuses primarily on the internationalization of economic processes and interests, starts out by addressing the issue of whether a transnational class of this kind is in fact rooted in the realities of society and is not merely a sociological construction. His arguments rest primarily on the global orientation of business, political, and professional elites that also finds expression in "similar lifestyles, particularly patterns of higher education (increasingly in business schools) and consumption of luxury goods and services" (Sklair 2001: 20). Jane Marceau, whose book bears the telling subtitle *The Making of an International Business Elite*, bases her thesis on the formation of an "international business class" on the results of a survey carried out among 2,000 graduates (from 12 countries) of the oldest and probably most renowned European business school, the INSEAD in Fontainebleau. She comes to the conclusion that the internationalization of business has changed the recruitment patterns for managers and that the sons of national upper and middle classes have responded to this development by attending business schools with an international focus. Here they not only learn the new management techniques they need to secure their old leading positions under the altered conditions that have emerged in their respective national economies, they are also trained with a view to making them the core of an "international business elite" (Marceau 1989a: 203–6; 1989b: 194, 208).

This focus on business schools is typical of the prognoses that see the end of the age of the national business elite. These business schools appear to be the training grounds of the new transnational business elite. The dominance of traditional institutions like the ENA thus appears drawing to a close, a development that is likely to spell the end of national patterns of elite recruitment. National elites, many observers conclude, must be seen as an outdated model, particularly in Europe, where traditions die hard.

The rapid development and growth of the MBA programs on offer in Europe would at first sight appear to point to both the global success and the internationalization of the Anglo-Saxon model of management training. The number of such MBA programs offered in Europe has almost doubled over the past few years. But if we take a closer look at the career successes of European business school graduates, we find that this impression rests on somewhat shaky ground. In fact, most of these successes have been achieved by management-consulting firms. At present MBAs play no more than a minor role in the top echelons of large industrial and financial corporations. In 1995 only 21 of the managing directors of the 100 largest British,

French, and German corporations held an MBA, 12 in British, seven in French, and only two in German companies. And in only one of these cases was the MBA the only higher academic title held by a manager. In all the other cases the MBA served simply to "top up" previous degrees earned at national elite institutions. Eleven of the 12 British top executives held degrees from Oxford or Cambridge, and all the French executives had earned a degree from one of the three leading Grandes écoles. And finally, this trend shows a downward tendency. With the exception of the two top German executives, none of these MBA holders belongs to the younger, post-1940 generation (Hartmann 1999: 120–1, 131). This impression is confirmed by data which show that only 59 of the 1,571 PDGs, heads of administrative councils, and company vice-presidents appointed in France in 1994 came from Fontainebleau, despite its reputation as the best business school in France, indeed in all of Europe (Byrkjeflot 2001: 152).

The relative insignificance of transnational MBA degrees might even lead us to believe that the internationalization of the top echelons of business is, on the whole, not so impressive after all. We find this hunch confirmed when we look at the 100 largest German, French, British, and US corporations. Only a very small number of top positions are held by nonnationals (two each in Japan and France, three each in Germany and the US, and seven in the UK), and the percentage of top executives with at least one year's experience abroad ranges only from 7 to 17 percent. The nonnationals who have made it to the top of large corporations all come from countries rooted largely in the same culture, e.g. Austria and Switzerland, both of which have majority German-speaking populations.

The fact is that the supposed internationality of "native" top executives must be seen as more fantasy than reality. This is particularly true of American CEOs. Only two of 97 have studied abroad and only six have spent a more or less protracted period of time abroad. For top careers in large US corporations, there would thus appear to be very little need to acquire any in-depth experience abroad. Closest to the Americans in this respect are the PDGs of large French corporations. By comparison, large German and British corporations have a relatively high percentage of top executives with experience abroad. But in these countries too the typical situation is that top executives spend large parts of their careers with the corporation they are later to head. Another striking fact is that most top executives with professional experience abroad have spent their time abroad in countries belonging to the same culture area or in countries with which their home country traditionally has good relations. If we include the remaining board members in the analysis, we find further confirmation of the meager level of internationality at the top echelons of major German companies. In the top 40 German companies nonnationals represent only 4 percent of board members, and only one in three board members has had any experience abroad. The picture is similar in the other leading industrialized nations. National career trajectories are clearly predominant there as well.

This statement applies to an even greater degree for politics, administration, and the judiciary. Although in creating the European Parliament, the European Commission, the various EU authorities, and the European Court of Justice, Europe has set some tangible signs for a Europeanization of these areas, and there is still a long way to go before we will be able to speak of the formation of a truly transnational elite. Europe's nation-states are still in charge of taking the majority of decisions bearing on careers in the highest-level European institutions. This applies to an even greater extent at the international level: despite the United Nations and the International Criminal Court, no real internationalization can be said to have taken place.

We can note in conclusion that at the international level there are as yet neither elite educational institutions in which upper- and upper middle-class children are socialized together nor is there sufficient transboundary (especially professional) mobility to provide for the homogeneity needed to create a common habitus. What is lacking is something that was typical of and common to the ruling classes of earlier great empires: a common culture and language which set the stage for an extensive or even complete integration of various regional and local elites into one class that ruled throughout an empire (Mann 1986).

Questions

1 In which way do the elite educational institutions in France, Great Britain, Japan, and the United States ensure the social reproduction of the national elites?

2 How important is money within the process of social selection?

3 What role does the class-specific habitus play for the elite recruitment in Germany?

4 Are there transnational elites?

6 Elites and class structures

Today the discussion on elites is clearly dominated by functionalist approaches. Although the classic positions of Pareto and Mosca, with their clear dichotomy of elite and mass, have again attracted growing attention in recent years, the functionalist view continues to define the approaches adopted by a large majority of theoretical and – especially – empirical studies. The credo here is: There are no longer any ruling classes or homogeneous elites; what we have today are competing, more or less equally powerful subelites that must be seen as open in social terms because access to them is determined mainly by individual performance, no longer by descent or social background. This, it is argued, is the reason why today the consensus among elites on which parliamentary democracy is predicated can no longer be established on the basis of social homogeneity but has to be sought by way of debate and competition among individual functional elites.

In view of the above-outlined process of elite formation in the major industrialized countries, an approach of this kind raises three central questions:

1 What role does performance really play in the recruitment of elites, and how socially heterogeneous are these elites?
2 Is it a fact that the business elite does not really enjoy a special position which enables it to exert considerably greater influence on the development of society than other groups?
3 What is the nature of the (inter)relationship between elites and classes within society?

6.1 Meritocratic elites and elite consensus

The empirical studies published on the career trajectories of top executives and politicians, high-ranking civil servants and judges in Germany, France, Britain, Japan, and the US call for more than a measure of skepticism with respect to the core statement of all functionalist elite theories, namely that access to subelites is based principally on performance. After all, highly selective social recruitment processes can be observed in all five leading industrialized nations; the large majority of elite positions are held by people from the upper middle classes or the upper class. Granted, there are differences between the individual countries – social origin, for example, tends to be somewhat more exclusive in France and Britain than in Germany or the US – as well as between the various sectors, with the business sector generally having the highest percentage of upper middle-class children and the political sector the lowest; but even so, none of these disparities have any pronounced influence impact on the general impression we gain. The important sectors of society (with a few exceptions, such as the German political elite) are clearly dominated by the upper-middle classes, indeed to a large extent by persons from an upper-class background.

Functionalist elite researchers who, on the whole, are aware of these facts, attempt to use two arguments to integrate them into the structures of their theories. First, they point out that the disproportions in social recruitment can be explained primarily by disparate academic achievements and as such are basically not in conflict with the performance principle as the key access criterion. While it is true that they do not deny the connection between social origin and the acquisition of academic titles, they still argue that this is accounted for primarily by disparities in performance and motivation. Dreitzel and Dahrendorf's remarks on this topic are symptomatic here. Second, based on the correlation found between education and professional career, and borrowing on classic modernization theories (Blau and Duncan 1967; Treiman 1977; Zapf 1971), they assume a clear-cut tendency toward more meritocracy, i.e. a social opening of elites. Existing links between social background and access to elites, they contend, have been loosened, if not completely broken, as a result of the reform and expansion of higher education.

At first sight, there is something to be said for both arguments; yet they do not bear up to closer scrutiny. If we take a look first at the correlation between academic success and access to elites, we find that there is clearly such a connection. Neither can we simply dismiss the argument that the exclusive academic qualifications generally required for top positions cannot be obtained without extraordinary achievements. For example, one in three of the approximately 30,000 (of over two million) US high school graduates who achieve 700 or more points on the verbal SAT, go on to one of the top ten universities, while a further 10 percent are accepted at one of the universities ranked among the highest 20 (Greene and Greene 2000: xxiii). However, even if we disregard the argument that social origins affect strengths and weaknesses in achievement, one fact remains: places at the sought-after elite institutions such as Harvard or Yale are not allocated purely on grounds of achievement. As noted in Chapter 5, the social background of candidates, defined in terms of the criterion "personality," plays a very direct and central role here. This is true of all exclusive educational institutions, be they the famous private universities in the US, the renowned

Grandes écoles, the distinguished public schools in the UK, or the top universities in Japan.

The importance of an upper- or upper middle-class background for access to elites can also be seen in Germany, where there are, as yet, no such elite educational institutions. The two international benchmark tests, PISA and IGLU, have demonstrated plainly that a good number of selection mechanisms in the German education system ensure that educational careers are also highly dependent on a child's social background, indeed in an even more broad sense than in most other countries. Germany's three-tier secondary school system plays a central role in this selection process. When decisions are made on what children should move on to preparatory schools, the key factors involved are not only superior – and background-related – performance of children from the upper strata of society but also teacher assessments of children, which are heavily colored by social origin. For instance, assuming equal performance levels, the child of an executive is (depending on the federal state concerned) two and a half to three times more likely to be recommended for attendance at a preparatory Gymnasium than a working-class child.

A child from the so-called "educationally remote strata" who, despite all these obstacles, reaches a university is then confronted with the extremely effective "unofficial" curricula and the behavior patterns of the "education-oriented strata." According to a study undertaken by the German Studentenwerk (Student Services Association), these students also have to cope with greater material problems. The proportion of such students who are obliged to take up regular employment in order to finance their studies is about twice as high as it is among other students. This is then reflected in the fact that twice as many of them take longer than average to complete their studies. All in all, the university prospects for children from working-class families or normal while-collar or civil service backgrounds are far worse than they are for children from the upper classes, despite the fact that universities have gone through a process of social opening. This, understandably, can be seen most clearly among those who acquire the highest degree offered at German universities, the doctorate. Almost half of those awarded a doctorate in the subjects most important for elite recruitment come from the upper and middle classes, which are thus vastly overrepresented.

If the premises on elite selection based on achievement should prove to be accurate, at least in principle, then the offspring of broad segments of the population that have earned a doctorate should have the same chances of reaching top positions as PhD holders who have grown up in upper- or upper middle-class surroundings. Since the doctorate is the highest academic qualification in Germany, and since, in the functionalist view, academic qualifications are the highest performance-related influencing variable and at the same time the most reliable indication of individual talent and effort, then PhD-holding children from working-class or white-collar families must have shown at least the same degree of ability and effort as their contemporaries from the upper classes. Indeed, there are good reasons to assume that it costs them a great deal more talent and diligence, because they have to start out by overcoming the numerous social obstacles facing them in their school and university careers. If their prospects of a top career are still worse than those of their peers from the upper classes, this can clearly have nothing to do with their ability and willingness to achieve.

Precisely this, however, is the case in large corporations, in business and trade associations, and in the highest-level courts, as is clearly documented by the study on the four PhD cohorts between 1955 and 1985 (Hartmann 2002). Not even earning the highest German academic title can come anywhere near making up for the handicap imposed by a non-middle-class background. Parental background, then, not only has an indirect impact on elite recruitment based on academic qualifications, it also has a very direct influence in terms of personality- and thus background-related selection criteria. This applies all the more, the greater the power associated with a given position: more for the top management levels of leading corporations or higher-level courts than for medium-sized companies or state-level federal courts. Keller is thus completely wrong when she states with respect to the business elite that the largest companies are the most advanced in terms of recruitment on a performance basis, regardless of social background (Keller 1963: 83). As a rule, the exact opposite the case.

If we at the same time consider the great significance attached to personality-related criteria in the admission procedures of elite educational institutions, we very soon find ourselves face to face with the basic weakness of the functionalist approach. This goes for Keller as well, even though she does provide us with a highly differentiated analysis in this regard. When she states in summary that, far from being hereditary, the crucial qualifications needed for advancement into elite positions can be attained only on the basis of individual personal achievement, she too is missing the central point of the matter (Keller 1963: 262–4). While individual achievement does indeed play a major role here, even if we disregard the social conditions bearing on achievement, we find that there is still a second career factor that is equally, or possibly even more, important, i.e. that of class-specific habitus, the acquisition of which is easily comparable with the factor of inheritance. A social background in the "better circles" still functions as a door opener to top positions.

This goes for Germany no less than it does for the other major industrialized nations. The only difference lies in the actual mechanisms involved. Whereas social selection in France or the US, for example, operates primarily by means of the admission procedures of the exclusive educational institutions, the German education system only serves as a rough preliminary filter in this process. In Germany much more of the decisive selection process is shifted to the course of a person's professional career. The effect is ultimately the same. Access to the important elites is largely reserved for the offspring of the upper-middle and – to an even greater extent – upper classes.

In certain respects the political sector is an exception to this rule. Here we do in fact find some major differences as regards the social origins of top politicians, because the structure of political parties may differ quite considerably from country to country. The extremes are represented by Germany on the one hand and France and Japan on the other. Whereas in Germany the selection process in the major popular parties has meant that candidates from the broad population have notably better chances of advancement than in other sectors of society,[1] in France and Japan the typical party structures, dominated as they are by dignitaries and clientelism, give clear preference to politicians with a middle-class background. It is not social proximity to the electorate but degrees from elite national educational institutions that determine whether or not aspirants are nominated as candidates for high political offices. What this means in effect is that the social background of the political elite differs relatively little from that of the business or administrative elite.

In view of such social recruitment practices, the question is of course whether functionalist elite theory is wrong – both in terms of its core thesis regarding socially heterogeneous meritocratic elites and in its assumption that consensus and cooperation among subelites is obstructed by the latter's functional specialization and autonomy no less than by heterogeneous social backgrounds. The situation in France and Japan militates, even at first sight, against any such premise. The two languages even have specific expressions for the very close relationships between the business, political, and administrative elites. In France the now common process by which high-ranking officials from government administration move into top positions in major companies is referred to as *pantouflage*,[2] and the people involved are called *catapultés* or *parachutes* (those have been catapulted upward or those who have parachuted down), because they have landed at the top instead of having to climb up the ladder of internal company hierarchies.[3] In Japan there is a very similar term for this process. It is termed "amakudari," that is, "those who have descended from the heavens."

More than half of the 100 largest French companies are headed by such men, 40 of them by former members of the famed Grands Corps. In Japan the same situation is typical for the financial sector, where one-time high-ranking MoF or Bank of Japan officials head one in four of the country's 150 largest banks. Such moves are less frequent in industry, though they are not uncommon. For instance, top figures from MITI later move on, almost without exception, to top positions in business (generally as presidents or vice-presidents of large corporations) (Cutts 1997: 197; Kerbo and McKinstry 1995: 95). The picture in the political sphere is similar. Approximately one in four members of the Japanese parliament and more than one in three prime ministers have previously held a high-ranking position in a ministry. Indeed, nearly two-thirds of French presidents and prime ministers over the last 30 years had previously been members of one of the administrative Grands Corps.

The close links between the personnel in administration, business, and politics are largely the result of the time such people have spent together in the country's exclusive elite educational institutions. Since graduates from these elite institutions are appointed to most top positions in all important spheres of society, moves from one sector to another do not constitute a problem. It ultimately makes no difference whether an Enarque, after a period at the Inspection des Finances, or a Todai graduate, after holding office in the MoF, moves to the top echelon of a major bank previously under his control or is appointed to a cabinet position. Be it here or there, he will be among people very much like himself. Having attended the same elite institutions, these people have known each other for years, irrespective of their fields of activity or political affiliations. This, combined with similar social backgrounds, provides the basis for a large measure of shared attitudes and behaviors. To cite an example, there is little doubt that the discreet discussions conducted directly between the Socialist government and the employers' associations in the second half of the 1990s were greatly facilitated by the fact that Socialist Prime Minister Jospin and the chairman of the French employers' association, at the same time CEO of the Wendel corporation, de Seillière – both ENA graduates – shared an office for three years as members of a Grand Corps in the French foreign ministry. If we further bear in mind the fact that almost all major positions are concentrated in the capital cities of Paris and Tokyo, we cannot fail to see that it is far less difficult than functionalists are fond of maintaining[4] for the elites from different sectors to forge a basic consensus.

The situation in the US is typified far more by close links between business and politics than by career moves by high-ranking administrative officials to the top echelons of other sectors. Over the last 30 years in particular, the number of cabinet members who have previously held top management positions in large corporations has grown to extraordinarily levels. Under President George W. Bush, this goes for nearly half of all the highest-ranking members of government, including Vice-President Cheney, Defense Secretary Rumsfeld, and Secretary of Commerce Evans. Constant moves from influential political offices to top positions in large corporations, and vice versa, are characteristic here.[5] Compared with Japan in particular, in the US we also find brisk and active exchange processes between politics and academia.[6] A man like the current President of Harvard University, Summers, Treasury Secretary under President Clinton, is no exception here. The present Secretary of the Treasury, Snow, was also once a university professor. Another factor further conducive to mutual understanding is the high percentage of graduates from elite universities active in all sectors.

In the UK, and above all in Germany, the various sectors of society are more clearly delineated, and moves by top staff from one sector to another are accordingly less common. Here only a handful of leading top managers have been previously active in high political or administrative office (Hartmann 1999: 129). While such moves between politics and business are becoming more frequent – as illustrated in Germany by Hamburg's Senator for Finance, Peiner, who once headed the Gothaer Insurance Company, or the new RAG Board Chairman, Müller, who is a former Federal Minister of the Economy – they still tend to be more or less rare. Careers like that of former German President Herzog are also still the exception; having held positions as professor, undersecretary, minister of a German state, supreme court justice, and, finally, as German President, Herzog was equally at home in the worlds of academia, administration, politics, and jurisprudence.[7]

Whereas the many years they spent together in public schools, at Oxbridge, or in the Guards, have enabled a large proportion of British elites to develop common behavior patterns and attitudes, and thus a solid basis for mutual trust and understanding, in Germany it is social background that forms the primary basis for cross-sectoral consensus. Furthermore, bearing in mind the fact that, due to the dominance there of large popular parties, the political elite in Germany is far more heterogeneous than it is, for example, in France, Japan, or the US, we may assume that the process of forging consensus among elites is more difficult and more time-consuming in Germany than it is in the other large industrialized nations.

6.2 The special role of the business elite

One of the most significant differences between the representatives of functionalist elite research (such as Dahrendorf, Dreitzel, Keller, and Lasswell) on the one hand and critical elite theorists (such as Bourdieu and Mills) on the other lies in their assessment of the influence of the business elite as compared with that of other elites. Bourdieu and Mills repeatedly point to the former's structurally conditioned predominance. In his early studies Bourdieu states quite clearly that economic capital is "at the root of all other types of capital" (Bourdieu 1983 [1986/1997]: 54), and in his more recent publications he still speaks of the markedly strong effects of the business sector. Mills is even more clear on this point. He goes as far as to describe the "chief executives" as "those who, by fact and by proxy, hold the power and the means . . ." and against whom "no powers effectively and consistently countervail" (Mills 1959: 125). Although Mills qualifies this very pronounced statement at another point, and even though Bourdieu's position is less pointed in his later works, the difference between their approach and the functionalist approaches is unmistakable. There can be no doubt that both Mills and Bourdieu see a special role for the business elite.

It is precisely this special role that is disputed by the representatives of functionalist elite research. Keller's arguments are the most systematic in this respect. In her book on *Strategic Elites* she uses the example of a conflict between U.S. Steel and US President Kennedy over a planned hike in steel prices to assert that the times are past in which, in pursuing its own interests, the business elite also appeared to be pursuing general national interests. The saying, What's good for U.S. Steel is good for the country, Keller argues, no longer holds true. She then goes deeper into the matter. Regardless of their importance, she argues, today economic goals are only one of a number of desirable goals. Thus the business elite is forced to compete with other elites for available resources. A country's economic performance generally constitutes only *one* measure of its social progress, and this one element must always be weighed up against other factors such as military strength, international prestige, mass education, or scientific success. Indeed, Keller goes a step further, criticizing even the manner, crimped in her eyes, in which Parsons assigns roles to given functions. She even questions the validity of his statement, made in connection with his AGIL paradigm, that one of the four functional imperatives of society, adaptation to the environment, is performed largely by business. For Keller, the military, the diplomatic sphere, and the academic sphere, to name only these, are likewise in charge of discharging key tasks in this connection (Keller 1963: 96–7). She thus explicitly rejects the notion that the business elite plays any pre-eminent role. Many other representatives of the functionalist approach assign to the political elite (implicitly or explicitly) the particular position of power which they refuse to accept for the business elite.

Today, however, a brief glance at the German media casts more than a shade of doubt on views of this stamp. Just about all political discussions and positions of topical interest in Germany today revolve around the supposed need to secure and bolster Germany as an attractive location for business.[8] Be it tax policy, the future of the social welfare system, the need to restructure Germany's university landscape, or the perspectives of scientific research, this issue is the central point of reference. This even extends into the terminology used. Students as paying customers of universities, business-style accounting systems in public administration, a new German Federal Labour Agency with a board chairman instead of the traditional Federal Employment Office,[9] run by a president, the (now common) practice of naming of football stadiums after their major sponsor – all these examples indicate, even for the cursory observer, how great the influence of the business sector has become on all spheres of society today.

A closer look at the situation, including a glance behind the façades, confirms this first impression, revealing a clear-cut structural imbalance in favor of the business elite, based primarily on this elite's exclusive power of decision over investments, rationalization measures, and, in the end, factory closures. The rapid internationalization of business structures has, over the past 20 years, noticeably increased the power that the business sector has always derived from its position in society – after all, not only the number of jobs available but also, to a large extent, tax revenues and the financial situation of social insurance agencies depend on decisions taken by business corporations. This makes it possible for the latter, but also to an increasing degree for medium-sized companies as well, to exert enormous pressure on all other spheres of society. Before they actually implement planned investments, for example, companies now almost routinely present the public sector with possible alternatives in an attempt to push through their own aims and wishes with respect to tax burdens, legal requirements, or subsidies. Whether these alternatives actually exist or not is in many cases wholly irrelevant. What counts is the political impact of such threats.

As the fierce competition for such investments clearly shows, local authorities no longer see themselves in a position to set down conditions of any kind for the companies in question. On the contrary, they outdo one another in promises of direct or indirect subsidies, provision of infrastructure services, or cooperation with local research institutes or universities. In spite of the huge financial problems facing them, municipalities seek to lure potential investors by offering them all manner of (legal, semi-legal, and at times illegal) concessions and benefits. Berlin, for instance, sought to lure the music corporations Warner and EMI from Hamburg and Cologne by offering them, in addition to subsidies to cover their building conversion costs, a maximum rent level of eight euro per square meter as well as worker orientation allowances of €10,000. Such offers have now become the usual procedure. Germany's federal states – indeed, even entire nation-states – are played off against one another, the motto being: If you're willing to pay, you can pick the music.

A similar development can be observed in tax policy. For many years now there has been, at the national and the international level, something on the order of a competition for the most attractive tax rates and models for businesses, sometimes with disastrous consequences for tax revenues and thus also for public services. Dramatic losses in municipal tax revenues, due in large measure to changes in corporate tax laws, and the subsequent catastrophic consequences for urban infrastructure (roads, schools, theaters, libraries, etc.) and public employment, are just one example. Businesses are feeling increasingly emboldened to act in this way. For instance, the managing director of the Infineon company, Schumacher, last year threatened to move the company to Switzerland for tax reasons, even though the corporation has only paid taxes for one year since it was created a good five years ago, and has received almost one billion euro in state subsidies just for deciding to locate in Dresden. Although nothing more has come of this threat so far, other cases show the extent to which the state is prepared to adapt its tax laws to suit businesses. Recent developments in tax rates on the sale of company stock is symptomatic. As a result of massive pressure from the business sector, one and the same finance minister first presented a new law securing large insurance companies tax exemptions for profits stemming from sales of their numerous shareholdings, and then, again after heavy protest, rescinded the provision originally attached to this law and stipulating, logically, that any losses incurred from such transactions would not be tax-deductible. What this means for the insurance companies is that they can continue to sell their blocks of shares tax-free, while their life-insurance subsidiaries, which would otherwise have been faced with tax payments of up to six billion euro, are able to receive tax abatements for the losses they incur. With the finance ministry pointing to Germany's attractiveness as a financial center, and at the behest of the insurance sector, what was adopted in the end – instead of the uniform, legally binding provision that was actually called for – was a tax provision that makes a mockery of both Germany's tax system and any normal sense of justice and equity. It is interesting to note that the initiative behind the planning of this proposed law came from Hamburg's Senator for Finance, Peiner, who, before moving into politics, was for many years board chairman of the Gothaer Insurance Company. Although a direct and personal intertwinement of politics and business is as yet more or less rare in Germany, all these examples, to which many others could be added, clearly demonstrate the extraordinary influence the economic elite of this country has on the making of political decisions.

The structurally conditioned pre-eminence of capital and its top representatives is also increasingly reflected in the direct influence exerted by the top echelons of Germany's large corporations. They seek out and are sought out by the federal government, and in particular by the chancellor. Such top-level talks are becoming the rule. This applies not only for economic issues but increasingly for noneconomic issues as well. At the beginning of 2004, for example, Chancellor Schröder convened a brainstorming summit on education and science, inviting not only scholars or education experts but – above all – well-known top executives and business consultants. The three scholars in attendance were outnumbered by more than two to one by the following representatives of the business world: the board chairmen of German Telekom, Lufthansa, Schering, and Siemens, Ricke, Mayrhofer, Erlen, and von Pierer, the ex-chairman and current member of the supervisory board of BMW, Milberg, and the vice-president of Germany's major industrial association (the BDI), Harting, and Roland Berger, ex-president of a major business consulting corporation.

In addition to the formal and informal contacts between the business and the political elite, there is a steadily and rapidly increasing number of lobbyists. The parliamentary manager of the SPD was quoted in an article in the weekly newspaper *Die Zeit* last October as saying that their number had "literally exploded" after the government's move from Bonn to Berlin. The same article states that a total of 4,500 passes, which grant the holders unhindered access to the offices of members of parliament, had been issued to such lobbyists, a figure which far exceeds the number of journalists possessing such passes. A highly effective network has developed here, due, among other things, to the fact that more and more ex-politicians, such as former Defense Minister Scharping or former State Secretary for Finance Hauser now work for consulting companies. Acts of parliament are no longer only influenced by intensive discussions between lobbyists and important ministerial or parliamentary officials, they are sometimes even directly initiated by such talks. Furthermore, the lobbyists sometimes even receive proposed bills before the members of parliament to enable them to make "alternative proposals."[10]

Developments in Germany give an idea of what the situation must be like in countries such as Japan or the US, where the ties between the business world and the world of politics are traditionally much closer than in Germany. In addition to the direct and indirect means of gaining influence on political decisions common in Germany, there is another key matter: the role played by financial support of politicians in their election campaigns. In Japan, at the beginning of the 1990s, the average cost of an election campaign was calculated at approximately ¥400 million (over €3 million) per LDP parliamentary seat; the major share of this sum was raised by businesses (Rothacher 1993: 29–30). The classic country for election campaign contributions, however, is the US, where, for example, as long ago as 1976, successful candidates for Senate seats spent an average of $610,000 on their election campaigns. In the following ten years this sum rose dramatically to $3 million, only to more than double again by the year 2000, when the figure reached $7.7 million. While a seat in the House of Representatives is a good deal cheaper, it still costs $840,000, twice the figure it had reached ten years ago. The reason why these sums have increased so enormously is that in 90 percent of cases it is the candidate who spends more money on his election campaign who ultimately wins. The total of the sums raised for Congressional elections increased from $659 million in 1992 to $1.05 billion in 2000, and the figure for presidential elections rose in the same period from $331 million to $529 million. George W. Bush alone, even without any primaries, will have a "war chest" of almost $200 million to fall back on. All of the ten largest contributors to these funds are large banks or investment companies, such as UBS or Merrill Lynch.

This was no different in the last election period in 2000. The financial and real-estate sectors paid out almost $300 million (in addition to over 200 million dollars spent on lobby work) in support for candidates. The money is either paid directly to the target candidates or, and this is more effective in view of the donation ceiling of $2,000, it is channeled via company employees and members of their families. Another increasingly popular approach is to give candidates indirect rather than direct donations, what is known as "soft money." This soft money now accounts for almost 20 percent of donations, considerably more than the official support provided by the state, which amounts to less than 10 percent. If we further bear in mind the fact that about three quarters of donations from individuals comes from people with annual incomes of more than $200,000, i.e. people who belong to the top 2 percent of the population, and that candidates themselves put their own money into their election campaigns on a scale approaching the official state support they receive, we cannot fail to miss the influence exerted by the business elite and the upper class on the filling of important political offices. The situation with respect to high-level judicial posts is similar. Since under the US system these jobs are usually elected posts, donations are coming to play an increasingly important role here as well.

Indeed, the rates of increase over the past ten years have been even higher than in the field of politics. To cite an example, in 1994 a successful candidate for the Michigan Supreme Court spent an average of $287,000 for his election campaign, and six years later this figure had risen to $1.3 million (Phillips 2002: 323–9).

This situation reminds many observers, including the Nobel laureate in economics, Paul Krugman, or Nixon's one-time adviser Kevin Phillips, of practices typical of the late nineteenth and early twentieth centuries. At that time, not only did one in three senators number among the country's approximate 5,000 millionaires, but seats in the Senate were regularly purchased by the major railroad companies. How prevalent this practice was can be seen in the fact that a motion was proposed at that time that aimed at removing all senators in possession of bought seats. The motion was rejected by the Senate with the argument that the body would in that case be without a quorum (ibid: 292–30). The alliance between business and political elite was at that time so close that the period, known as the "Gilded Age" in a term coined by Mark Twain, became a synonym for the almost unrestricted power of large corporations and millionaires as well as for widespread political corruption. How remunerative donations to election campaigns can be for businesses today is demonstrated not only by the awards of contracts after the end of the Iraq war but also by the legislation of the past 20 years aimed at deregulating the American financial markets or providing tax relief for businesses. Even though major legislation can clearly not be explained solely in terms of direct financial benefits to politicians and intensive lobbying by industry and trade associations, and has had far more to do with the structural supremacy of capital, the effectiveness of donations and lobbyists should not be underestimated.

It is, in any case, more expedient to weigh up the influence of the business elite on the "basis of a number of key decisions," as recommended by Beyme (Beyme 1971: 203), rather than to seek to explain the effect on the basis of network analyses, as functionalist-oriented studies tend to do. Any attempt to determine the relative weight of the various sectoral elites by looking into their most important contacts and partners when it comes to solving cross-organizational problems is bound to suffer from a number of weaknesses. Two of them are crucial. First, many functionlist authors deliberately fail – and this is occasionally acknowledged (for instance by Higley *et al.* 1991: 47) – to analyze specific positions of power on the basis of the practical impacts of decisions or of criteria other than membership in the elite circles under study. It is simply assumed that these circles have a relatively egalitarian structure. Second, the central position of the political elite established by the findings of a given study is frequently predetermined by the way in which the problem under consideration is formulated. Typical of this approach is Hoffmann-Lange's comparatively precise and theoretically grounded evaluation of a Mannheim survey conducted in 1981. She concludes that the "representatives of the political-administrative system," with their share of over 50 percent, play a key role in the central circle of the elite, and she is only being logically consistent when she points to the "central role played by the political sector" (Hoffmann-Lange 1992: 386–7, 403–4). However, if we take a closer look at the central question involved in the survey, we find that this finding is anything but surprising. If we start out by asking an interviewee about the one field in which he has sought most intensely to "influence political decisions or public opinion," following up by asking him to name his most important contacts in this endeavor, then the question itself will necessarily prompt a response in which politicians are named high up on the list. This is not the way to determine where true influence lies.[11]

Here the only possible approach is to look into decisions of central importance. Even if we disregard company-related decisions that may have substantial impacts on whole regions or even countries (for instance, large-scale company mergers), though they are generally made by top management, without consulting with or informing others in advance, we cannot possibly overlook the dominance of the business elite even on immediately political decisions. Tax policy is a good example here in that it provides the financial basis for any state's capacity to act, and as such is the central element behind all political action. In the US, the pioneer of capital-friendly tax policies, the share of corporate taxes in total tax revenues has declined radically over the past few decades, i.e. during a period when the tax burden of the general population has risen sharply. About 30 years ago the level of income and social security tax (FICA) revenues was roughly the same as that of corporate tax revenues; recent figures show a relation of 3:1, despite a four- to fivefold increase in corporate profits over the past two decades (Phillips 2002: 149–50). In addition to the multitude of opportunities corporations have to cash in on loopholes in tax law, this development has been influenced primarily by the Reagan administration's tax reforms. The situation in Germany is similar. In the period from 1970 to 2000 the share accounted for by income tax in overall tax revenues has doubled, while the share accounted for by corporate and business taxes has declined by more than one-half. Since the year 2000 there has been a further massive reduction in corporate tax revenues, a fact which is reflected in the complaints of many local authorities over shortfalls in corporate tax payments, or even the need to refund taxes to corporations. Between 2000 and 2002 taxes on profits from incorporated companies (Aktiengesellschaften) and limited companies (GmbHs) fell from almost €24 billion to just over €3 billion.

However, tax reform has not only benefited corporations, it has also worked in favor of those in high income-tax brackets and large property owners. While real incomes (after taxes) fell slightly in the US for average wage earners between 1977 and 1999, the incomes of the top percent have more than doubled, reaching a figure of over $500,000 today.[12] In the 1990s alone their share of national income rose from 8.2 to 16.3 percent, with the result that these persons now earn more than the bottom 40 percent of the population. The top 0.1 per mill, that is, about 13,000 families, alone account for 3 percent, while the bottom fifth earns no more than 5 percent. If we look at assets, these inequalities are even more glaring. The top 1 percent now owns over 40 percent of all assets, twice as much as at the end of the 1970s. They own over 60 percent of business assets and bonds and one-half of all share and trust assets, and the top five per mill own almost one third of all shares and almost half of all bonds.

Tax policy has played an important role in this concentration of income and assets. The greatest effect was certainly achieved by the Reagan administration's reduction of the top income-tax rate from 50 percent to just under 30 percent. This, however, was only the extension of a broad trend that had been observed since the 1970s. Whereas in the 1960s the effective tax rate for the top 1 percent of society was six to seven times higher than it was for the average American family, by 1980 this figure had been reduced to a ratio of 3:2, and over the subsequent ten years the ratio was to reach a level of 1:1 (Henwood 1998: 67; Krugman 2002; Phillips 2002: 96, 121–4, 129, 150; Werner 2003: 31). George W. Bush has recently effected a further drastic reduction in the tax burden of rich US citizens and corporations by pushing through tax cuts amounting to $550 billions, and one of the core goals of his program is to halve, and ultimately abolish (by 2007), the tax on stock dividends. In 2001 he also signed a law designed to wholly abolish the inheritance tax, which has already been reduced several times, by the year 2011. This would most benefit the top per mill of the population, who at present account for more than half of the $20 billion in revenues stemming from this particular tax (Beckert 2003: 137–8).[13]

The overall picture in Germany is generally similar, although, thanks to a lack of statistical data, we have to rely more on estimates here.[14] Less than 0.1 per mill of the working population, that is, a grand total of 3,000 people, account for almost 2.3 percent of all income, a proportion similar to that in the US (Becker and Hauser 2003: 241). The top 1 percent of the population owns a good quarter of all German wealth, according to the *German Wealth Report*, a study published by the investment bank Merrill Lynch and the consultants Cap Gemini Ernst & Young – a very high proportion of the total, though not quite comparable with the US. The top 0.1 per mill alone, the 3,700 so-called "ultra-high net-worth individuals," own a share of 7.9 percent. The tax policies of the Kohl and Schröder governments have played an important role in this concentration of income and wealth, for example with their abolition of the wealth tax (Vermögenssteuer) and the marked reduction in the tax rate for the highest tax bracket which accompanied it.

Tax legislation is a good indication of the enormous influence wielded by the business elite on key political decisions. The interests of this elite are largely identical with those of the upper classes in general. Both stand to gain double benefits from these tax reforms. First, their personal income is taxed at a considerably lower rate, and second, thanks to the reduction in their tax burden, corporations are able to pay out more of their profits, and this in turn mainly benefits the upper classes and top executives. In the last 20 years the latter have succeeded in dramatically increasing their incomes, in the US from 50 times to 400 times an average worker's earnings. The record is held by Larry Ellison, head of Oracle, who managed to earn over $700 million in 2001. The gulf in Germany, where top earnings are "only" 100 times those of workers' earnings, is not as wide, but the trend is the same. In the period from 1997 to 2002 alone, the board members of the 30 DAX-listed companies have succeeded in raising their remuneration by about two-thirds. DaimlerChrysler leads the field here. On average its board members are paid €3.7 million in cash, excluding the comprehensive stock options they are offered. As an individual, the board spokesman of the Deutsche Bank, Joseph Ackermann, topped the list with an income in 2003 of about €11 million. He was able to increase his income by almost 60 percent over the previous year. With such incomes, the top executives of Germany's leading corporations are among the top 0.1 per mill of all income earners in Germany.

The comprehensive stock options provided to them in addition to salaries mean that board members themselves are important shareholders. For example, if all Daimler Chrysler board members were to cash in on their options, almost 10 percent of the company would belong to them. The most important executives at the Deutsche Bank, the Group Executive Committee, already own over 7 percent of their company's shares. In no way, then, can we speak of a control by corporate management in the sense meant by Burnham, and there are plainly and simply no conflicts of interest between managers and capital owners.[15]

6.3 The ruling class and power relations in society

The enormous concentration of productive wealth in the hands of a few per mill of the population, the levels of board-member incomes, and the tax reforms which benefit this circle more than any other illustrate not only the close ties between business elite and upper classes, with their enormous influence, these developments also permit us to draw some general conclusions on the relationship between elites and classes. This includes the connections between individual elites and the links between these elites and the upper classes, not to forget the relationship between class structures in society and the influence of elites on society.

If we start out by looking at the relationships between individual elites, we find that in all major industrialized countries there has been marked growth in the interdependencies among the key elites in business, politics, and administration, as well as, to a lesser extent, in the judiciary and the media. In countries like France and, less markedly, in Japan and the US, this process is already relatively far advanced. True, there are still different elite positions, but the fact that a considerable proportion of those in such positions regularly make career moves to other sectors means that the boundaries between the individual elites are blurring to an increasing extent. This is particularly the case in present-day Italy. In the person of Silvio Berlusconi this process of amalgamation has reached a dimension which only 20 years ago would have been decried as a particularly distorted caricature born of leftist propaganda. Presumably, hardly anyone could, at the end of the 1980s, have conceived that the richest man in one of the world's largest industrialized nations could at the same time be head of government and hold control over both the country's privately and publicly owned television networks. Such a concentration of power in the hands of a single person would at that time have been equally as inconceivable in an industrial society as the possibility that a parliament might pass laws which so obviously benefit the economic interests of this one particular person. Even though the spontaneous impression may be somewhat deceptive – this blatant amalgamation of public and private interests is increasingly meeting with resistance, for instance in the refusal of Italian President Ciampi to sign two laws which would have secured Berlusconi a large measure of immunity from criminal prosecution and served to further strengthen his media empire, it clearly indicates the close nature of the ties between the individual subelites on the one hand and between these elites and the upper classes on the other.

This, however, brings us face to face with the question of whether the concept ruling class is in fact closer to reality than the strict rejection of the term by functionalist elite research and the tentative use of the concept made by Mills and (more recently) Bourdieu would suggest. Keller gives the most precise summary of the arguments of functionalist elite theorists when she distinguishes between the "ruling class" and "strategic elites." In Keller's view what distinguishes a ruling class from an elite is that the former is far broader and more durable, its activities are less specialized, membership is less optional, and that its members share not only their professional and functional positions but also have a set of general habits, customs, and cultural behavior patterns in common. Its members are recruited from families with more or less monopolized access to the most important elites and who are able to pass down their advantages to the next generation. All this, Keller contends, distinguishes ruling classes fundamentally from elites, which are specialized in given sectors and display a tendency toward functional autonomy, since, in her view, no one person would be able to hold elite positions in more than one sector at one time. Elites are, she argues, recruited on the grounds of their individual skills and performance, which are no longer bound to specific social origins. As long as the core group was mainly recruited from a small and exclusive circle, i.e. the upper class, it was difficult if not impossible to distinguish between strategic elites and the class from which most of their members originated. In this age of a modern, functionally differentiated and specialized society, however, even the core group is forced to specialize, a development which has served to make access to individual elites relatively open in social terms. There is no longer one pyramid with one apex but a number of pyramids, each with its own elite at the top (Keller 1963: 57–60, 83).

If we look at the important elites in large industrialized nations from the point of view of these criteria, we find a number of good reasons to speak of the existence of a ruling class. Although Keller's basic distinction between elites and ruling class is analytically correct, in reality the boundaries are becoming increasingly blurred. Even if Berlusconi, bringing together several top offices in his person, is excluded from the analysis as a particularly extreme case, there are still a considerable number of people who hold elite positions in various sectors, many of them nearly at the same time. US Vice-President Cheney, for example, did actually give up his position as CEO of Halliburton for his term of office, but when his term is up he is more than likely to return there. Regular changeovers between various elite positions, known as *pantouflage* in France and *amakudari* in Japan, point in the same direction. There is, in any case, no convincing reason to speak here of a clear distinguishing line between individual elites. Furthermore, a large propor-tion of key elites have one thing in common: their backgrounds in upper-middle and (more importantly) upper-class milieus. Assuming the form of a class-specific habitus, this background ensures that they will have the same or similar "habits, customs, and cultural behavior patterns." It is not only their "professional and functional positions" that they share. The central role played by an upper middle-class or upper-class habitus in elite recruitment shows plainly that access to elite positions is far less open than Keller and the entire field of functionalist elite research maintain. The benefits of an upper middle-class or upper-class habitus are passed on from generation to generation, roughly in the same way that material benefits are passed down. Even if we ignore differences in background-related school and university achievements and degrees, what counts in gaining access to important elites is not only – indeed often not even primarily – individual performance. After all, the growing complexity of modern industrial society does not automatically entail any functional autonomy of individual elites, nor, in fact, do the "communication problems of the business and political elites" cited by Behme as his principal argument in rejecting Mills' concept of the power elite (Beyme 1971: 206).

The business elite of course seeks to ensure that it is adequately represen-ted in the political elite. As Beyme correctly notes, the influence of the "economically powerful" cannot be measured in terms of the number of people who seek to directly "articulate" such interests "in the state's power apparatus," because this group also has other means of achieving this end; however, the "overrepresentation of certain socially powerful strata and groups" increases their chances of influencing the power apparatus from the outside, because overrepresented groups act as influence "facilitators" (Beyme 1971: 220–1). Even in Germany key political positions are for this reason occupied by members of the business elite, or at the least by members of the upper classes. At present this applies not only for high offices in the cabinets of state governments ruled by the CDU/CSU and FDP but also for the Red-Green governments in power in Berlin and the state of North Rhine-Westphalia), where the interior ministry and the finance ministry are headed by sons of a steel works CEO and a regional court president, respectively.

All in all, today it is quite difficult to distinguish clearly "between the strategic elites and the class from which most of their members are recruited." There are good reasons to proceed neither on the premise of a system of competing pluralist subelites, as the functionalist elite theorists do, nor of a power elite in Mills' sense. Instead it would appear to make more sense (borrowing on a definition provided by Giddens) to proceed on the assumption of a diluted variant of the concept ruling class, namely the "governing class." For Giddens, a governing class of this kind is characterized by relatively closed social recruitment (mainly from the upper class) and a relatively high degree of integration. This class is distinguished from the classic "ruling classes" chiefly by the clear limitations set to its power by the fact that it is controlled (more or less) from below: its holders are forced to pay due regard to the population at large (Giddens 1974: 5–9).

If Giddens' thoughts are taken further, then, the term ruling class can be taken to mean not simply bourgeoisie, upper-middle class, upper class, or classe dominante in Bourdieu's sense.[16] Instead, the ruling class must be seen as made up of – and here we would be well advised to heed Mills' criticism of any assumption of an overly direct link between economic power and political rule – a circle of people recruited mainly from the key elites and the core of the upper-middle to upper classes. This group includes neither all members of the important elites nor all members of the upper classes, because the fact that someone holds a top position or stems from an upper-class family is simply not sufficient to justify membership in it. If one is really to belong to the ruling class, one must be permanently embedded in it, and in this way be in a position to exert significant influence on the development of society.[17]

There are three different ways to achieve this. First, a person may hold a top position for such a long period of time that he or she is successfully integrated into this class, irrespective of social origins. Politicians like Helmut Kohl in Germany belong to this category, whereas ministers of German state or federal governments (in particular SPD members) from ordinary parental backgrounds who serve only, say, one term in office and then return to their former professions or become ordinary members of parliament do not. The second means is to belong to the ruling class by birth. This path, however, is open only to a very small circle of heirs to very large estates (for example, the children of former German industrialist and majority BMW shareholder Herbert Quandt) who belong to the business elite simply by dint of the capital they own. This path normally remains closed to the son of a regional court president or chief physician; he will first have to hold a top position on his own merits, at least for a certain period of time. This, then, is the third variant. A person may find access to the ruling class if he or she holds a top position for a more or less brief period of time and then turns to a lower-level leadership position – provided this person was born into an upper middle-class or (preferably) upper-class family. This is the best short cut on the path to integration.

The most powerful individual group within the ruling class consists of the major representatives of capital, that is, the top executives of the large corporations and the most important shareholders and entrepreneurs. But not even they are always able to realize their interests directly. The current discussion on German education policy is a good illustration of this point. German capital appears to have nothing to say (despite sporadic initiatives by organizations representing the skilled trades) about Germany's three-tier system of secondary education – a system that seems anachronistic by international standards – even though this system must be seen as the main factor responsible for the serious weaknesses of the German school system in terms of both performance and social equity. Here it is regarded as important to show proper consideration for those sections of the upper and upper-middle classes and one-time lower-middle classes who view the process of early selection involved as an important competitive advantage for their children. The reason behind this is that the support of these sections of the population is needed for other reform projects important to business interests, primarily the dismantling of the social security system.

Generally speaking, and this is the blind spot of most elite theories and studies, the successes and failures of the business elite, as well as of the entire ruling class, depend largely on the power relations in society as a whole. The ongoing radical reforms of tax laws illustrate this point very clearly. On the one hand, reforms on this scale have only been possible because potential opposition forces in parties and – above all – in labor unions, had already been substantially weakened by other developments. There have been two key processes at work here. The internationalization of the economy and the associated – real or supposed – comprehensive new options it has opened up for capital have markedly reduced the influence of both unions and left-wing or classic social-democratic parties and organizations.[18] The effect of this development, which has been underway since the late 1970s, was boosted substantially after 1989 by the collapse of what was known as "real socialism." The dramatic weakening of the unions, including a decline in membership over the last 30 years from – in many cases – 50 percent to a level of 10 percent or lower in the US and France – or the rapid demise of the only *real* social alternative to capitalism – were the factors that set the stage for the seemingly unstoppable offensive of neoliberal ideas and concepts in politics.

On the other hand, changes in German tax laws, which constitute a core, if not *the* core element of this allegedly unstoppable development, serve both to cement and further consolidate this shift in power relations in German society. The ongoing discussion in Germany on the need for longer weekly working hours in the public sector illustrates this point very clearly. The reason cited by the German state governments for the need to increase working hours from 38.5 to 42 hours a week is that they lack sufficient tax revenues. This development, however, is largely a result of the tax policies pursued over the past 20 years. Should the authorities actually succeed in pushing through this drastic increase in working hours, private companies will inevitably follow suit in due course. This would again lead to a shift in the balance of power in society to the detriment of the population at large, further increasing the scopes of action open to the ruling class.

All these changes also have a massive influence on the balance of weight between the individual German elites, and they clearly favor the business elite to the detriment of the political elite. As Mills clearly demonstrates in his "Power Elite" with reference to the New Deal, the political elite inevitably has a relatively large amount of influence and leeway when social movements and forces are able to curb the power of capital. But it is precisely the opposite that has occurred over the past few years. Business has been dictating the frameworks for major political decisions, with the consequence that the independent influence of politics is on the wane. The parliamentary process is playing an increasingly smaller role in the making of political decisions, which are influenced more and more by the ways in which they are "staged" by the media (Sunday evening political talk shows on television instead of parliament as the principle arena for political discussion), expert commissions (like the so-called Hartz and Rürup commissions in Germany), and actions taken by trusts such as the CHE (the Bertelsmann Trust's Center for University Development), and the Conference of University Chancellors (Rektorenkonferenz), which may been seen a quasi-unofficial ancillary ministry of education and science. With counterforces in society having lost a good deal of their influence, and parliament being increasingly sidelined on important issues, decision-making processes are coming more and more to be concentrated in small circles. The business elite prefers to make central decisions in intimate circles together with a handful of compliant politicians. The disciplinary instruments available to the parties in parliament are then brought to bear to mobilize the parliamentary majorities needed.

This has triggered a downward spiral that is further and further weakening the political parties. It is commonly argued that if politics lacks the clout it needs to shape the course of events, it will in the end have no choice but to follow, for better or for worse, the laws of the world market – a development that is bound to spell the end of any broad-based political engagement. The huge drops in the membership in the large German popular parties – in the 1990s the CDU lost over a fifth of its members, the corresponding figure for the SPD being over one-quarter – are clear indicators of this trend, as is the continuous decline in electoral turnouts in all major industrialized countries. In the US the turnout for even the most important elections is never higher than 40 percent (for Congressional elections) or nearly 60 percent (for presidential elections). All a candidate now needs to become president of the United Sates is to secure the votes of less than one-quarter of the registered electorate.

This has one further consequence. Since turnout figures vary substantially as a function of income and education levels, the influence of the well-to-do and the rich is also growing accordingly. According to data from the U.S. Census Bureau, the upper quarter of the working population who possess a university degree (bachelor or higher), and thus have incomes between one and a half and three times as high as the average, have a turnout of almost 80 percent, whereas the bottom 20 percent, with a maximum of three years' high school education, turn out to vote at rates of only about 30 percent. What this means in effect is that the top quarter accounts for five times as many actual voters (about 36 percent) as the bottom fifth (just over 7 percent). If we take this one step further, we see that winning the votes of the top 25 percent is close to sufficient to be elected president of the US. It can at any rate be said that it is far more important to cater to the interests of this group than to those of the bottom half of the population, which is hardly ever able to mobilize as many voters as the former group. This social imbalance among the electorate is an additional factor serving to consolidate the influence on politics of the business elite and the upper class.

The overall development in the US, and not at all only in the US, can be accurately characterized in the words of Warren Buffett, the second richest man in the world, who summed up the situation in his 2004 annual share-holders newsletter as follows: "If class warfare is being waged in America, my class is clearly winning." Those who, like Keller and the rest of her mainstream functionalist colleagues, pin their hopes on the insight of elites when it comes to creating better living conditions (Keller 1963: 279), defining the role of the general population, the so-called mass, in this process as a largely passive one, are, it would seem, victims of an illusion. The ruling class will as a rule turn to its account whatever opportunities are offered it by the state of the power relations in society.

Questions

1   What role does performance play for the recruitment of elites?
2   How socially heterogeneous or homogeneous are the elites?
3   Does the business elite enjoy a special position which enables it to exert considerably greater influence on the development of society than other elites?
4   What is the nature of the relationship between elites and classes within society?
5. Is there a ruling class today?

Notes

1 Introduction

1 On this point, see Chapter 2.
2 In recent years a more markedly dichotomous worldview has shown signs of gaining increasing popularity among members of the academic middle classes in Germany. This is illustrated by a number of comments made during the course of the ongoing discussion on elite universities in Germany. The Vice-Chancellor of Heidelberg University, Karlheinz Meier, made a point typical of this tendency when he sought to underscore his call for the right of universities to select their own students by remarking, "Elite and mass are not compatible."
3 See Chapter 3 for further details.

2 Elite and mass

1 Gustave Le Bon (born in Nogent-le-Routrou in 1841, died in Paris in 1931) was originally a doctor before he began, after the Franco-Prussian war of 1870/1871, to devote himself intensively to the field of anthropology. He published several ethnologically oriented books on earlier and non-European cultures, including the Arab and Indian civilizations, and then went on to delve into ethnopsychology and, finally, mass psychology.
2 He was able to profit from two studies with a criminological focus which had been published shortly beforehand, one by Gabriel Tarde (*The Laws of Imitation* 1890) and the other by Scipio Sighele (*The Delinquent Masses* 1893), which dealt – without initially acknowledging the fact – with the behavior of masses (Dingeldey1964: XX).
3 In his book *Masse und Geist* (1984) Berking uses the example of German sociology in the Second German Reich and the Weimar Republic to demonstrate how important this has been for the emergence and further development of sociology.
4 Gaetano Mosca (born in Palermo in 1858, died in Rome 1941) originally worked in the legal profession before becoming a professor in Turin in 1898. From 1923–1933 he taught in Rome. Beside his scholarly work he was also actively involved in politics, as a member of the Italian parliament, as an undersecretary in the Italian Ministry of the Colonies (1914–1916), and as a senator (from 1919).
5 A second edition, published in 1923, was enlarged to include six additional chapters. Most of today's translations are based on this edition. The American translation of 1939 was entitled *Ruling Class* and the German post-Second World War was *Die herrschende Klasse*.
6 Despite his highly critical view of the parliamentary system, Mosca was still one

of its foremost defenders. As he very clearly put it in his chapter on parliamentarism, "the defects of parliamentiary assemblies, and the evil consequences which their control of power and their participation in power produce in all representative systems, are merest trifles as compared with the harm that would inevitably result from abolishing them or stripping them of their influence" (Mosca 1896 [1939]: 256). Mosca remains essentially faithful to this view in the six new chapters which he wrote three decades later. On the one hand, he admits a considerable shift in his stance, now pleading for greater forbearance toward the "parliamentary regime;" on the other hand, though, he also reaffirms his earlier view on minority rule, according to which "every system of government which claims to rest on the will of the majority embodies an untruth" (§ 8; omitted in Mosca 1939).

7 In addition to money, Mosca sees science, or the occupations based on, it as a new social force which only "up a certain point [to] counterbalances the material prestige of the rich and the moral prestige of the clergy" (ibid.: 145).

8 Here Mosca specifically rejects the positions held by representatives of this view, including racial ideologists and the theoretical trailblazers of the ideology of National Socialism, Gobineau and Gumplowicz (ibid.: 62).

9 See also ibid.: 340–1.

10 See also ibid.: 129.

11 Vilfredo Pareto (born in Paris in 1848, died in Céligny near Geneva in 1923) came from an old Genoese family. After working as an engineer and the general director of a commercial enterprise, and following an unsuccessful candidacy for election to the Italian parliament, Pareto turned his attention increasingly to science. His original interest was in economics, and in 1893 he took over Walras' chair in economics at the University of Lausanne, where he published, among other studies, a standard work on income distribution. Over the years he became more and more interested in sociology. He published several studies on sociology before he came into a substantial inheritance and was able, in 1907, to give up his professorship in order to devote himself entirely to his work on his "Trattato." He declined to accept the honorary senatorship which Mussolini bestowed upon him shortly before his death.

12 The present study cites paragraph (§) instead of page numbers because the various translations and editions differ considerably in their selection of texts from the complete transcript of the "Trattato;" it is hoped that this will aid the reader in finding his or her way through the text.

13 This does not, however, mean that it is less contradictory. In this respect there is little difference between the two authors. Both Pareto's and Mosca's analyses contain numerous contradictions and logical jumps or breaks. See here, among others, Hamann 1964 and Hübner 1967.

14 Here, however, Pareto here is primarily concerned with residues. His discussion of the connection between the derivations and the circulation of elites is thus briefer.

15 Eisermann speaks of emotional structures (Eisermann 1987: 143), Bach of universal sociomental structures (Bach 1999: 101), and Hamann of the constant, irrational core of social acts (Hamann 1964: 6).

16 This somewhat lapidary argumentation leaves a number of questions open. What is meant by "sufficiently large" and how, precisely, this situation may come to pass is at best inferred indirectly, and with a measure of good will on the reader's part, from Pareto's argumentation as a whole. The reasoning here is not really systematic.

17 A summary of the most important arguments can be found in Michel's essay in the "Archiv für Sozialwissenschaft und Sozialpolitik" published in 1908 (Michels 1908).

18 Robert Michels (born in Cologne in 1876, died in Rome in 1936) came from an old Cologne merchant family. In 1901, having completed his studies, he went to Rome, where he joined the Socialist Party. On his return to Germany he joined the Social Democratic Party (SPD). In 1907 he left the Italian Socialist Party. After teaching appointments at universities in Belgium and France, Michels, now an Italian citizen, was appointed professor of political economy and statistics at the University of Basle in 1914. In 1922 Michels joined the Italian Fascist Party, and five years later, on Mussolini's initiative, he was given a professorship at the University of Perugia.

19 Like Mosca and Pareto, Michels asserts that all ruling classes endeavor to bequeath their power to their descendants (Michels 1911: 13).

20 Michels later abandoned this position and became an open proponent of Italian fascism.

21 Although it must be conceded that some of the inconsistencies in Pareto's and in particular Mosca's terminology are certainly due to the translations, and that Mosca himself rejected Pareto's concept of "elite" as too imprecise to describe his political class (Mosca 1896 [1939]: 450, FN [omitted in Mosca 1939]), this must still be seen as criticism.

22 While – unlike Michels – Mosca and Pareto were able to resist the immediate enticements of fascism (two major reasons being that they were considerably older than Michels and that they both held a secure professional position), they must unquestionably be counted among those who paved the way ideologically for the rise of fascism.

3 Functional elites

1 Karl Mannheim (born in Budapest 1893, died in London 1947) was brought up in a wealthy Jewish family. After studying in Budapest, Freiburg, Berlin, Paris, and Heidelberg, he was appointed to a professorship at the University of Frankfurt am Main in 1930, but in 1933 he was forced to emigrate to London, where he first taught at the London School of Economics and in 1942 became a professor at the University of London.

2 After completing his studies at the University of Chicago Harold D. Lasswell (born in Donellson, Illinois, in 1902, died in New York in 1978) was first appointed Professor at Milikan University, later at Chicago, at Yale and, finally, Harvard.

3 The second point also applies for Lasswell's later studies which otherwise focus theoretically more on functional subelites (Lasswell 1948; Lasswell and Lerner 1965, etc.).

4 An important exception here is Mills and his "Power Elite," which is dealt with in more detail in Chapter 4.1.

5 For further details on this second point, see Bachrach 1966: 26–8.

6 The term veto groups coined by David Riesman in his book *The Lonely Crowd* (1953) was generally used to designate elites that seek mutually to curb the powers of other elites.

7 Robert Dahl (born in Inwood, Iowa, in 1915) studied at Yale, where he was later appointed professor.

8 Domhoff's (1978) empirical examination of Dahl's study criticizes precisely this point and reaches wholly different conclusions with respect to the distribution of power and political influence in the case of the urban renewal.

9 Thus it is not particularly surprising that Dahl's later works are increasingly critical of the role of business as regards public welfare, and that he points to the structural imbalance in its favor (Dahl 1982).

10 This is also true of other European authors such as Aron, who deals explicitly with the relationship between elite and class (Aron 1950; 1960).

11 Otto Stammer (born in Leipzig in 1900, died in Berlin in 1978). Having completed university training, Stammer worked from 1930–1933 as a political journalist and as an official adviser on cultural affairs to the German Social Democratic Party (SPD) in Breslau. Following a period of politically imposed unemployment and some later work in the pharmaceutical industry, he held a position after the war at the University of Leipzig before being appointed, in 1951, to a professorship at the Free University of Berlin, where he remained until the end of his career.

12 He includes in his criticism not only conservative authors such as Ortega y Gasset and his *Revolt of the Masses* but also Mannheim and his complaints about the massification of society and its consequences for the process of elite formation (Stammer 1965a: 64–5).

13 Ralf Dahrendorf (born in Hamburg in 1929) is the son of an SPD member of the Reichstag. After competing his studies, he was appointed to a professorship at the Academy of Social Economics (Akademie für Gemeinwirtschaft) in Hamburg in 1958. Following this he took up posts as professor at the Universities of Tübingen and Constance. In 1969 he was appointed parliamentary state secretary in the German Foreign Office, and in 1970 EEC Commissioner. From 1974 to 1988 he was director of the London School of Economics, from 1991–1997 vice-chancellor of the University of Oxford, and since 1993 he has been a member of the British House of Lords.

14 For a further definition of elite, see Stammer's extremely compact definition in his article for the *Wörterbuch der Soziologie* (*Dictionary of Sociology*) (Stammer 1969).

15 The central role of social conflict, which for Dahrendorf is more a matter of power than of ownership structures, clearly distinguishes Dahrendorf's theoretical approach from the equilibrium models of both Parsons and Pareto, as Dahrendorf expressly notes describing his approach (Dahrendorf 1967: 273). For further information concerning the approach as a whole, see Dahrendorf 1967: 263–77 and 1987: 39–56.

16 Dahrendorf's pupil Wolfgang Zapf proceeds in a similar manner. He does almost entirely without any precise definitions. In his opinion it is possible to use, for "linguistic" and other reasons, the concepts upper strata, leadership groups, and elites "synonymously" (Zapf 1965b: 10). According to Zapf, to be more precise, the term upper strata should be used as a "collective term for all positions of high prestige and income," while the terms leadership groups and elites should be reserved for "the small group of persons within the upper strata who influence decisions on matters of wide social import" (Zapf 1965b: 10). Zapf himself, however, fails to heed this advice in his own purely empirical studies (Zapf 1965a, b, c).

17 This assessment is sharply criticized by other functionalists. In the view of Hoffmann-Lange, for example, this does not even apply to Dahrendorf's prime example, Germany, other than for a relatively short period after the Second World War (Hoffmann-Lange 1991: 98–9).

18 Hans Peter Dreitzel (born in Berlin in 1935) was appointed to a professorship at the Free University of Berlin after completing his studies at the University of Göttingen.

19 Dreitzel agrees with Dahrendorf on the point that the disproportionate recruitment of elites from the upper strata and upper middle classes is due to the educational privilege these strata enjoy; this fact cannot, though, be explained by the lesser financial resources available to the working class, and is in essence

bound up with the fact that these strata themselves are less "education-oriented." Referring to the 1950s, Dahrendorf explicitly states that one could say "with only a slight degree of exaggeration" that "every working-class family in the Federal Republic of Germany could afford a university education for at least one child" (Dahrendorf 1962: 22). He at that time, logically, hoped that educational reform would bring about fundamental change in elite recruitment.

20 At another point Dreitzel puts this very clearly when he says, "Fully developed industrial society is characterized by the fact that the values associated with achievement and progress (and thus also the norms of professional performance) generally tend to prevail" (ibid.: 152).

21 Suzanne Keller (born in Vienna in 1930) attended Hunter College and Columbia University, taught at Princeton, MIT, and Brandeis University, and was appointed to a professorship at Princeton in 1968.

22 A summary of the major elements of her analysis can be found in Keller's article "Elites" in the *International Encyclopedia of the Social Sciences* (Keller 1968).

23 Parsons is of the opinion that four basic functions must be fulfilled in all systems: adaptation to changing environmental situations, the definition and realization of goals, integration of the various components of the system, and basic pattern maintenance (Parsons 1959 and Parsons and Smelser 1956).

24 Rebenstorf is the only scholar to have dealt at length with the various theoretical approaches from Mosca to Bourdieu; see her book *Die politische Klasse*, which appeared two years earlier (Rebenstorf 1995).

25 Hoffmann-Lange is the only scholar to have attempted, in her postdoctoral thesis (Hoffmann-Lange 1990, largely identical with Hoffmann-Lange 1992), to deal in somewhat greater detail with the theoretical base of the 1981 survey (Wildenmann *et al.* 1982). This is, however, an exception in German elite research, which has been clearly dominated over the past three decades by political scientists. Any theoretical advances which may have been made, as in the case of Herzog (1975, 1982, 1990) or von Beyme (1971), have focused primarily on the professionalization of political carriers and hence also of elites. Consensus between elites is also a pivotal problem for Herzog and Beyme. Herzog specifically states that the professionalization of political careers has a marked influence on politicians' willingness to reach a consensus, since an "esprit de corps," that is, there is a "sense of community among political professionals" which transcends party barriers (Herzog 1975: 226). The question of whether and to what extent other elites are included in this consensus reached by the political elite remains an open one.

26 Her summary is the only publication in the context of the four large-scale elite surveys that seeks, more or less comprehensively, to refer the empirical results back to the initial theoretical issue of elite consensus and to discuss these results on this basis.

27 Hoffmann-Lange claims that in democratically constituted societies "it is realistic to assume close correspondence between formal and actual power structures" (Hoffmann-Lange 2003: 117) and is not in line with reality. The greatly enlarged scopes for action and decision-making which the much-touted phenomenon of globalization has, in the past two decades, meant for economic elites in their dealings with political institutions clearly illustrates this point.

4 Elites and classes

1 A summary of the most important results can be found in Mills' article in the *British Journal of Sociology* (Mills 1959).

2 C. Wright Mills (born in Waco, Texas in 1916, died in New York in 1962) was

the son of an insurance representative. After studying at the Texas Agricultural and Mechanical College, the University of Texas, and the University of Wisconsin, Mills held positions at the University of Maryland and Columbia University in New York. Politically, he was initially close to politics of the New Deal and later to the emerging New Left.

3 In this context Mills criticizes the studies on the upper echelons of local small-town society which assume that their findings are transferable to the country as a whole, noting that it is not possible to simply "add up [these classes] to form a national upper class" (ibid: 45). This would be tantamount to completely overlooking their hierarchical structure.

4 See also ibid.: 165–70 and 209–10.

5 Pierre Bourdieu (born in Denguin, Béarn, France in 1930, died in Paris in 2002) was the son of a post office clerk. After studying at the renowned École Normale Supérieure (ENS) he worked at the University of Algiers, the Sorbonne in Paris, and the University of Lille, before being appointed in 1964 to a position at the prestigious École Pratique des Hautes Études (today École des Hautes Études en Sciences Sociales). In 1981 he was appointed professor of sociology at the Collège de France, France's most renowned scientific institution. Parallel to his scholarly work, Bourdieu was politically active on the side of the left.

6 When we speak here of Bourdieu we should bear in mind that many of his analyses and publications were not conducted by Bourdieu alone. Colleagues such as Jean-Claude Passeron, Luc Boltanski, and, above all, Monique de Saint Martin worked together with him on the majority of his studies on the reproduction mechanisms of the ruling class. Even though she is not given credit as co-author of the book, *La Noblesse d'Etat*, she did participate in the writing of two chapters, and thus of 50 percent of each of two of the four major sections, and she also co-authored the first version of an additional section.

7 Whereas in his early works Bourdieu spoke almost exclusively of the "dominant class," he discards this concept almost entirely in *La Noblesse d'Etat* (1989a) in favor of the concept "field of power," in order, as he says, to break with the substantialist view of things, which he sees as being as typical for Marxism as it is for functionalism (Bourdieu 1989a [1996]: 263–4). Despite this change in terminology, *La Noblesse d'Etat* rests largely on earlier publications, and indeed sometimes even reproduces them word for word (for example, Bourdieu and de Saint Martin 1978).

8 In the above-mentioned interview with Wacquant, Bourdieu remarked that generally "in most of today's developed societies . . . the transmission of power – including economic power – is more and more dependent upon possession of educational credentials" (Bourdieu 1993b: 27).

9 The German translation says more appropriately "a veiled form of siphoning off profits."

10 Krais and Gebauer (2002) provide a very good and at the same time compact explanation of Bourdieu's habitus concept.

11 Bourdieu also refers to habitus as a "socially constituted system of structured and structuring dispositions acquired in practice and constantly aimed at practical functions" (Bourdieu and Wacquant 1992/1992: 121).

12 "The tendency toward self-reproduction of the structure is realized only when it enrolls the collaborations of agents who have internalized its specific necessity in the form of habitus and who are *active producers* even when they consciously or unconsciously contribute to reproduction. Having internalized the immanent law of the structure in the form of habitus, they realize its necessity in the very spontaneous movement of their existence" (Bourdieu and Wacquant 1992: 140).

13 This direct concurrence between habitus and field is said to occur above all in the economic field (Bourdieu and Wacquant 1992 [1996]: 162).

14 Bourdieu also calls this elite "nobility" or "*consecrated* elite" (Bourdieu 1993b: 28; original italics).

15 The growing interlinkages between large corporations as well as their increasing financial dependence on banks is of greater benefit to the graduates of Sciences Po and ENA than it is to Polytechnique graduates (Bourdieu 1989a [1996]: 325–7).

16 This is why the social exceptions, "sucess stories" as Bourdieu calls them, are often the most resolute and best defenders of the elite schools (Bourdieu 1993b: 30).

17 In an earlier version Bourdieu and de Saint Martin spoke of intelligence as the one feature in which all claims to legitimacy are "accumulated" (Bourdieu and de Saint Martin 1987: 27).

18 This distribution, it is noted, by no means follows mechanical principles. A banker's son could doubtless become a professor of law, and the son of a professor of medicine a top-ranking civil servant in a ministry (Bourdieu 1989a [1996]: 335).

19 Bourdieu sees this difference as fundamental to all ruling classes (Bourdieu 1993b: 24ff; 1989a [1996]: 264ff).

20 Here we find in Mills' work salient chords that bear clear resemblance to the classic dichotomy of elite and mass.

21 For Bourdieu, this is a naively Machiavellian view.

22 Bourdieu always insists that the actual danger he sees stems not only from the side of "economism" but also from "semiologism (nowadays represented by structuralism, symbolic interactionism, or ethnomethodology), which reduces social exchanges to phenomena of communication and ignores the brutal fact of universal reducibility to economics" (Bourdieu 1983 [1997]: 54).

23 The very different national conditions involved certainly explain part of the differences between Bourdieu and Mills, who both focus primarily on their own (French and US) national situations.

5 National education systems and elite recruitment

1 The *classes préparatoires* are two-year preparatory classes for the entrance examinations to the Grandes écoles; they are provided at about 800 lycées.

2 For further details, see Hartmann 1997.

3 In 1995 Bac C was renamed Bac S.

4 The upper class includes big industrialists, members of company boards, large landowners, senior civil servants, and generals; the upper middle classes, i.e. the rest of the bourgeoisie, include major entrepreneurs, executives, senior civil servants and officers, and professionals.

5 The alumni of this school call themselves Exonians, borrowing on the British term Etonians. For the traditional east coast upper class, graduation from one of the leading private schools such as Phillips Exeter or Groton frequently counts for more than a degree from Harvard or Yale (Dye 1995: 173). A member of the upper class describes the reason for this and what he sees as the principle function of the exclusive east coast schools in the following words: "In fact, for many of us in Old Money families, class institutions served virtually all the functions of the ideal 'affective' middle-class family, teaching us everything from self-respect to sexual hygiene" (Aldrich 1996: 274).

6 The three most famous American universities, Harvard, Yale, and Princeton, have admission rates of about 10 percent.

7 These selection standards are essentially the same as those characteristically used in the recruitment of top executives in Germany. See Hartmann 1996, 2001a, 2002.

8 Beside the eight Ivy League universities – Harvard, Yale, Princeton, Columbia, Pennsylvania, Brown, Cornell, and Dartmouth – this includes the equally or almost equally well-known universities Stanford, MIT, Johns Hopkins, Chicago, Northwestern, and Carnegie Mellon.

9 The leading elite universities are somewhat better represented in the big New Economy corporations. Of the 13 largest companies, seven are headed by men who studied at one of the top ten universities, namely Harvard, Princeton, Stanford, or MIT or CalTech.

10 The situation in the New Economy provides some grounds for this assumption. Of the ten largest companies, seven are headed by the sons of professors, architects, doctors, or senior managers. The fact that, for the first time in many years, a member of the Ford family has been appointed CEO of the Ford Motor Company is a further indication of this tendency.

11 In the 1993 entrance examinations more than half the secondary preparatory schools asked questions which could not be answered on the basis of the typical high school curricula (Cutts 1997: 159).

12 Post-doctoral theses (*Habilitationsschriften*) are of little significance outside of universities and the medical profession.

13 Since the figure fell from 61 to 54 percent between 1975 and 1985 (Hartmann 2002: 57), and assuming this development has remained relatively constant, it ought now to lie below 50 percent.

14 In the case of the upper classes it should be remembered that the survey was dealing with generations of fathers up to the beginning of the 1960s. Generally speaking, a good share of upper civil servants and academically trained professionals today no longer stem from the upper-middle classes. See Hartmann 2002: 35–43 for more details.

15 Elite in the broad sense includes members of the top echelons in companies with more than 150 employees, politicians with the rank of mayor of an important major city or, in Germany, ministers of at least a German federal state, members of the legal profession from vice-presidents of regional or superior regional courts, and university professors.

16 None of the PhD holders covered here was a member of the Federal Constitutional Court.

17 In addition to social background, age at commencement of studies, and possible stays abroad, these include length of studies, subject of study, and place of study (Hartmann 2002: 77–9, 86).

18 In a recent interview with *Manager Magazin* on the occasion of his nomination to the publication's hall of fame, a German executive who wielded substantial influence for decades, Günter Vogelsang, described the significance of a good general education as follows: "If a potential top executive is unable to associate anything with the dates 1066 and 1077, is questionable whether this person's view of the world is suitable for a management position."

19 This rule decides on careers in the large popular parties, the CDU/CSU and the SPD. Due to their different party structures and voter clientele, this rule does not apply fully to the FDP or the Green Party.

20 Whereas PhD holders from the upper-middle and upper classes hold two to three times the number of top positions in the business sector (excluding business associations, which are not dealt with in any detail here) as compared with similar positions in politics, law, or academia, the majority of successful PhD holders from the broad population are to be found in these three sectors.

21 For the situation in the 1980s see also Hartmann 1995.
22 The 1985 cohort, incidentally, presents just the opposite picture. Thanks to improved career opportunities in the business sector, children from the upper and middle classes have withdrawn from the judiciary. The share they now account for has declined by a figure almost twice as high as that for their peers from the broad population.
23 The opposite conclusion reached by the Potsdam elite study (Schnapp 1997a: 77; 1997b: 106) has a number of technical flaws and thus does not reflect reality. In the first place, the 33.6 percent coverage rate for all companies outside the financial sector is very low. Second, as regards the financial sector, institutions such as the German central bank (Deutsche Bundesbank), the state central banks (Landeszentralbanken), cooperative banks, savings and loan associations (Bausparkassen), and publicly owned social insurance companies were included, even though their top management positions tend to be filled according to political criteria, not by the standards customary in the private sector. And third, some of the people interviewed in banks, but also in other companies (for example, deputy vice-chairmen of supervisory boards) do not really belong to the true business elite. The fact that one in four persons counted here as members of the business elite is at the same time a member of a labor union makes this more than clear.

6 Elites and class structures

1 See Chapter 5, Section 5.5.
2 There is no adequate English translation for this term.
3 Career moves from business to politics are far more rare, but they do occur. An example of this is the French Minister of Financial and Economic Affairs, Mer. Originally, he was a typical "*parachuté.*" After attending the École Polytechnique and working for a time at the Corps des Mines, he moved to an industrial corporation, Saint Gobain, where within a short space of time he became managing director and later PDG. Subsequently he was appointed to the same position with the newly merged steel corporation Usinor Sacilor. In being appointed minister, he has now switched his field of activity once again.
4 This spatial concentration also makes it easier to involve intellectuals, as is shown by the example of Paris, where certain clubs play this role.
5 This does not, though, apply for the leading corporations. Cheney proves to be the exception here.
6 Such switches are also frequent in France. In Raffarin's present cabinet three ministries (defense, youth and culture, and education and research) are headed by former professors.
7 However, the new German president, Horst Köhler, has a similar career to show. Köhler held positions as department manager and state secretary at the federal state and national level, was president of the German Association of Savings Banks (Sparkassen- und Giroverband), the European Bank for Reconstruction and Development, and the IMF before becoming German President.
8 The debates underway in other countries are similar in nature.
9 The first board chairman of the new German Federal Labour Agency, Florian Gerster, failed, among other reasons, because he mistakenly believed that the new term designating his position meant that he could actually act like a real board chairman of a large corporation. The terminology borrowed from the business world is also leaving its mark on the agency's day-to-day work. An example of this is a new directive entitled "Business Policy 2003, Objective: Reduction of Unemployment." These instructions require advisory teams of four

or five placement people to produce every month 60 cases of a first failure to register (consequence: nonpayment of unemployment benefits for a set period of time) and seven cases of a second failure to register (consequence: loss of unemployed status).

10 For more information on the growth of lobbyism in Germany, see Leif and Speth 2003.

11 An additional point is the overrepresentation of politics in the survey samples. In the light of the fact that 40 percent of the elite members selected for the Potsdam elite study came from the political and administrative spheres and only a good 22 percent from the business field, and that the disparity in the interviews actually conducted was even greater (43 to 18 percent), it is clear that the sample alone accords considerably greater weight to the political sector.

12 Even within this top percent, income distribution is extremely disparate. More than one third of growth in incomes was accounted for by the top 0.1 per mill of this group, who have an average annual income of $17 million (Krugman 2002).

13 It is also interesting to note that tax audits have shifted more and more from the rich to the poor. Whereas in 1988 11.4 percent of those who earned over $100,000 were audited, and only 1.03 percent of those who earned less than $25,000 faced the same procedure, by 1999 these figures had been radically reversed, the present ratio being 1.15 to 1.36 percent (Phillips 2002: 327).

14 See Bergmann 2004.

15 This applies in relation both to large private shareowners and trusts. While there are differences, it turns out, surprisingly, that, looked at in terms of manager remuneration, the growing influence of trusts actually favors salary increases at the management level (Höpner 2003: 148–9).

16 Bourdieu's *classe dominante* is far too large. In contrast to the terms upper-middle class or upper class, it includes wide circles of the salaried intelligentsia.

17 See Krais 2001 on the relationship between elites and ruling class.

18 How effective alleged new options – which in reality do not even exist – in fact are is demonstrated by the relentlessly reiterated argument that the top executive need to be paid drastically more to prevent them from moving on to other countries. Even though this option is in fact as good as nonexistent since the market for top executives has proven resistant to internationalization, this argument is still wielded effectively and has had an influence that should not be underestimated on the enormous salary increases given to executives, for the simple reason that nobody has publicly examined its validity. The picture is similar with regard to the current heated discussion on the relocation of jobs to eastern Europe. Contrary to publicly expressed declarations and assertions, though, this is, as least at present, no more than a marginal phenomenon. Experts on eastern Europe estimate that fewer than 50,000 jobs have been lost by Germany to countries in eastern Europe since 1990. The common argument that wages for less qualified jobs are bound to decline sharply because of a worldwide oversupply of the skills concerned is likewise a matter of heated controversy among experts (Goldthorpe 2002).

Bibliography

Adonis, A. and Pollard, S. (1997) *A Class Act. The Myth of Britain's Classless Society*, London: Hamish Hamilton.

Aldrich, N.W. (1996) *Old Money. The Mythology of Wealth in America*, New York: Allworth Press.

Armengaud, A. (1986) "Die Rolle der Demographie," in F. Braudel and E. Labrousse (eds), *Wirtschaft und Gesellschaft in Frankreich im Zeitalter der Industrialisierung. 1789–1880. Bd. 1*, Frankfurt a.M.: Syndikat, pp. 126–73.

Aron, R. (1950) "Social structure and the ruling class," *The British Journal of Sociology* 1: 1–16 and 126–43.

—— (1960) "Classe sociale, classe politique, classe dirigeante," *Archives Européennes de Sociologie* 1: 260–82.

Bach, M. (1999) "Vilfredo Pareto," in Kaesler, D. (ed.), *Klassiker der Soziologie. Bd. 1. Von Auguste Comte bis Norbert Elias*, Munich: C.H. Beck, pp. 94–112.

Bachrach, P. (1966) *The Theory of Democratic Elitism. A Critique*, Boston: Little, Brown and Company.

Barberis, P. (1996) *The Elite of the Elite*, Ipswich: Ipswich Book.

Bauer, M. and Bertin-Mourot, B. (1996) *Vers un modèle Européen de dirigeants? Comparaison Allemagne/France/Grande Bretagne*, Paris: C.N.R.S. et Boyden Executive Search.

Becker, I. and Hauser, R. (2003) *Anatomie einer Einkommensverteilung. Ergebnisse der Einkommens- und Verbrauchsstichproben 1969–1998*, Berlin: Sigma.

Beckert, J. (2003) "Demokratische Umverteilung: Erbschaftsbesteuerung und meritokratisches Eigentumsverständnis in den USA," in W. Fluck and W. Werner (eds), *Wie viel Ungleichheit verträgt die Demokratie? Armut und Reichtum in den USA*, Frankfurt a.M.: Campus, pp. 119–43.

Benzner, B. (1989) *Ministerialbürokratie und Interessengruppen. Eine empirische Analyse der personellen Verflechtungen zwischen bundesstaatlicher Ministerialorganisation und gesellschaftlichen Gruppeninteressen in der Bundesrepublik Deutschland im Zeitraum 1949–1984*, Baden-Baden: Nomos.

Bergeron, L., Furet, F. and Kosseleck, R. (1969) *Das Zeitalter der europäischen Revolutionen 1780–1848. Bd. 26. Fischers Weltgeschichte*, Frankfurt a.M.: Fischer Verlag; Lizenzauflage (1998) Augsburg: Weltbild Verlag.

Bergmann, J. (2004) "Die Reichen werden reicher – auch in Deutschland. Die Legende von den moderaten Ungleichheiten," in I. Artus and R. Trinczek (eds), *Über Arbeit, Interessen und andere Dinge*, Munich and Mehring: Rainer Hampp Verlag, pp. 57–75.

Berking, H. (1984) *Masse und Geist. Studien zur Soziologie in der Weimarer Republik*, Berlin: Wissenschaftlicher Autoren-Verlag.

Beyme, K. von (1971) *Die politische Elite in der Bundesrepublik Deutschland*, Munich: R. Piper & Co.

Blau, P.M. and Duncan, O.D. (1967) *The American Occupational Structure*, New York: Wiley.

Bock, H.M. (1999) "Republikanischer Elitismus und technokratische Herrschaft," in M. Christadler and H. Utterwedde (eds), *Länderbericht Frankreich*, Opladen: Leske + Budrich, pp. 381–403.

Bottomore, T.B. (1993) *Elites and Society*, 2nd Edition, London: Routledge (1st Edition 1963).

Bourdieu, P. (1974) "Avenir de classe et causalité du probable," in *Revue française de sociologie* 15: 9–42; Ger. "Klassenschicksal, individuelles Handeln und das Gesetz der Wahrscheinlichkeit," in P. Bourdieu, L. Boltanski, M. de Saint Martin and P. Maldidier (1981), *Über die Reproduktion sozialer Macht*, Frankfurt a.M.: EVA, pp. 169–226.

—— (1979) *La distinction, Critique sociale du jugement*, Paris: Éditions de Minuit: Engl. *Distinction. A Social Critique of the Judgement of Taste*, Cambridge, Mass.: Harvard University Press 2004 (original printing 1984/1986).

—— (1980) *Le sens pratique*, Paris: Éditions de Minuit; Engl. *The Logic of Practice*, Stanford: Stanford University Press 1990.

—— (1983) "Ökonomisches Kapital, kulturelles Kapital, soziales Kapital," in R. Kreckel (ed.) *Soziale Ungleichheiten. Soziale Welt*, Sonderband 2. Göttingen: Otto Schwartz & Co.: 183–98; Engl. "The (three) forms of capital," in J.G. Richardson (ed.), *Handbook of Theory and Research in the Sociology of Education*, New York & London: Greenwood Press 1986, pp. 241–58 (Reprint in A.H. Halsey, P. Brown and W.A. Stuart (eds), *Education, Culture, Economy, and Society*, Oxford: Oxford University Press 1997, pp. 46–58).

—— (1984) *Homo academicus*. Paris: Éditions de Minuit; Engl. *Homo academicus*, Cambridge: Polity Press 1988.

—— (1989a) *La noblesse d'Etat. Grandes écoles et esprit de corps*, Paris: Éditions de Minuit: Engl. *The State Nobility. Elite Schools in the Field of Power*, Cambridge: Polity Press 1996.

—— (1989b) *Satz und Gegensatz. Über die Verantwortung der Intellektuellen*, Berlin: Wagenbach Verlag.

—— (1991) "Das Feld der Macht und die technokratische Herrschaft," in I. Dölling (ed.), *Die Intellektuellen und die Macht*, Hamburg: VSA-Verlag, pp. 67–100.

—— (1992) "Die feinen Unterschiede," in M. Steinrücke (ed.), *Die verborgenen Mechanismen der Macht*, Hamburg: VSA-Verlag, pp. 31–47.

—— (1993a) *Soziologische Fragen*; Engl. *Sociology in Question*, London: Sage Publications.

—— (1993b) "From ruling class to the field of power," an interview with Pierre Bourdieu on "La Noblesse d'État," *Theory, Culture & Society* 10: 3, 19–44.

—— (1994) *Raisons pratiques. Sur la théorie de l'action*, Paris: Seuil; Engl. *Practical Reason: On The Theory of Action*, Cambridge: Polity Press 1998.

—— and Boltanski, L. (1975) "Le titre et le poste: rapports entre le système de reproduction," *Actes de la recherche en sciences sociales*, 2/3: 95–108; Ger. "Zum Verhältnis von Bildung und Beschäftigung," in P. Bourdieu, L. Boltanski, M. de

Saint Martin and P. Maldidier, *Über die Reproduktion sozialer Macht*, Frankfurt a.M.: EVA, 1981, pp. 89–116.

—— and Passeron, J.C. (1964) *Les héritiers. Les étudiants et la culture*, Paris: Éditions de Minuit, Engl. *The Inheritors. French Students and their Relation to Culture*, Chicago: University of Chicago Press 1979.

—— and Passeron, J.C. (1971) *Die Illusion der Chancengleichheit*, Stuttgart: Klett.

—— and Saint Martin, M. de (1978) "Le patronat," *Actes de la recherche en sciences sociales*, 20/21: 2–82.

—— and Saint Martin, M. de (1982) "La sainte famille. L'épiscopat français dans la champ du pouvoir," *Actes de la recherche en sciences sociales* 44/45: 2–53.

—— and Saint Martin, M. de (1987) "Agrégation et ségrégation. Le champ des grandes écoles et le champ du pouvoir," *Actes de la recherche en sciences sociales* 69: 2–50.

—— and Wacquant, L.J.D. (1992) *Réponses pour une anthropologie réflexive*, Paris: Seuil; Engl. *An Invitation to Reflexive Sociology*, Chicago: University of Chicago Press.

—— Boltanski, L. and Saint Martin, M. de (1973) "Les stratégies de reconversion. Les classes sociales et le système d'enseignement," *Social Science Information* 12: 61–113, Engl. "Changes in social structure and changes in the demand for education," in S. Giner and M. Scotford-Archer (eds), *Contemporary Europe. Social Structures and Cultural Patterns*, London: Routledge and Kegan Paul 1977, pp. 197–227.

Bürklin, W., Rebenstorf u. a., H. (1997) *Eliten in Deutschland. Rekrutierung und Integration*, Opladen: Leske + Budrich.

Byrkjeflot, H. (2001) *Management Education and Selection of Top Managers in Europe and the United States*, Bergen: LOS-Center Rapport 0103.

Chevallier, J. (1997) "L'élite politico-administrative, une interpénétration discutée," *Pouvoirs. Revue Francaise d'etudes constitutionelles et politiques* 80: 89–100.

Cookson, P.W. and Persell, C.H. (1985) *Preparing for Power. America's Elite Boarding Schools*, New York: Basic Books.

Cutts, R.L. (1997) *An Empire of Schools. Japan's Universities and the Molding of a National Elite*, Armonk: M.E. Sharp.

Dahl, R. (1961) *Who Governs? Democracy and Power in an American City*, New Haven: Yale University Press.

—— (1964) *Power, Pluralism and Democracy: A Modest Proposal*, Paper for the annual meeting of the American Political Science Association, Chicago, September 9–12.

—— (1982) *Dilemmas of Pluralist Democracy*, New Haven: Yale University Press.

Dahrendorf, R. (1961) *Gesellschaft und Freiheit. Zur soziologischen Analyse der Gegenwart*, Munich: R. Piper & Co.

—— (1962) "Eine neue deutsche Oberschicht? Notizen über die Eliten der Bundesrepublik," *Die neue Gesellschaft* 9: 18–31.

—— (1965) *Gesellschaft und Demokratie in Deutschland*, Munich: R. Piper & Co.

—— (1967) *Pfade aus Utopia. Arbeiten zur Theorie und Methode der Soziologie*, Munich: R. Piper & Co.

—— (1972) *Konflikt und Freiheit*, Munich: R. Piper & Co.

—— (1987) *Fragmente eines neuen Liberalismus*, Stuttgart: Deutsche Verlags-Anstalt.

Dargie, C. and Locke, R. (1999) "The British Senior Civil Service," in E.C. Page and V. Wright (eds), *Bureaucratic Élites in Western European States*, Oxford: Oxford University Press, pp. 178–204.

Dingeldey, H. (1964) "Zur Einführung," in G. Le Bon *Psychologie der Massen*, Stuttgart: Alfred Kröner, pp. xiii–xxiii.

Domhoff, G. W. (1967) *Who Rules America?* Englewood Cliffs: Prentice-Hall.

—— (1971) *The Inner Circles*, New York: Viking.

—— (1978) *Who Really Rules? New Haven and Community* Power *Reexamined*, New Brunswick and London: Transaction Books.

—— (ed.) (1980) *Power Structure Research*, Beverly Hills: Sage.

—— (1983) *Who Rules America Now? A View for the '80s*, Englewood Cliffs: Prentice-Hall.

—— and Dye, T.R. (ed.) (1987) *Power Elites and Organizations*, Beverly Hills: Sage.

Dreitzel, H.P. (1962) *Elitebegriff und Sozialstruktur. Eine soziologische Begriffsanalyse*, Stuttgart: Ferdinand Enke.

Dülmen, R. van (1982) *Entstehung des frühzeitlichen Europa 1550–1648. Bd. 24. Fischers Weltgeschichte*, Frankfurt a.M.: Fischer Verlag; Lizenzauflage (1998) Augsburg: Weltbild Verlag.

Dye, T.R. (1976) *Who's Running America?* Englewood Cliffs: Prentice-Hall.

—— (1979) *Who's Running America? The Carter Years*, Englewood Cliffs: Prentice-Hall.

—— (1983) *Who's Running America? The Reagan Years*, Englewood Cliffs: Prentice-Hall.

—— (1985) *Who's Running America? The Conservative Years*, Englewood Cliffs: Prentice-Hall.

—— (1990) *Who's Running America? The Bush Era*, Englewood Cliffs: Prentice-Hall.

—— (1995) *Who's Running America? The Clinton Years*, Englewood Cliffs: Prentice-Hall.

Edwards, T., Fitz, J. and Whitty, G. (1989) *The State and Private Education: An Evaluation of the Assisted Place Scheme*, London: The Falmer Press.

Eisermann, G. (1987) *Vilfredo Pareto. Ein Klassiker der Soziologie*, Tübingen: Mohr Siebeck.

Euriat, M. and Thélot, C. (1995) "Le recrutement social de l'elite scolaire en France," *Revue française de sociologie*, 36: 403–38.

Feldman, P.H. (1988) *Recruiting an Elite*, New York: Garland Publishing.

Field, G.L. and Higley, J. (1980) *Elitism*, London: Routledge and Kegan Paul.

Giddens, A. (1974) "Elites in British class structure," in P. Stanworth and A. Giddens (eds), *Elites and Power in British Society*, Cambridge: Cambridge University Press, pp. 1–21.

Goldthorpe, J.H. (2002) "Globalisation and social class," in *West European Politics* 25: 3, 1–28.

Greene, H.R. and Greene, M. (2000) *Inside the Top Colleges. Realities of Life and Learning in America's Elite Colleges*, New York: Cliff Street Books.

Hamann, R. (1964) *Paretos Elitentheorie und ihre Stellung in der neueren Soziologie*, Stuttgart: Gustav Fischer.

Hartmann, M. (1990) *Juristen in der Wirtschaft. Eine Elite im Wandel*, Munich: C.H. Beck.

—— (1995) "Bank lawyers: a professional group holding the rains of power," in Y. Dezalay and D. Sugarman (eds), *Professional Competition and Professional Power. Lawyers, Accountants and the Social Construction of Markets*, London: Routledge.

—— (1996) *Topmanager – Die Rekrutierung einer Elite*, Frankfurt a.M.: Campus.

—— (1997) "Die Rekrutierung von Topmanagern in Europa. Nationale Bildungssysteme und die Reproduktion der Eliten in Deutschland, Frankreich und Großbritannien," *Archives Européennes de Sociologie* 38: 3–37.

—— (1999) "Auf dem Weg zur transnationalen Bourgeoisie? Die Internationalisierung der Wirtschaft und die Internationalität der Spitzenmanager Deutschlands, Frankreichs, Großbritanniens und der USA," *Leviathan* 27: 113–41.

—— (2000) "Class-specific habitus and the social reproduction of the business elite in Germany and France," *The Sociological Review* 48: 241–61.

—— (2001a) "Klassenspezifischer Habitus oder exklusive Bildungstitel als Selektionskriterium? Die Besetzung von Spitzenpositionen in der Wirtschaft," in B. Krais (ed.), *An der Spitze. Deutsche Eliten im sozialen Wandel*, Konstanz: UVK, pp. 157–215.

—— (2001b) "Bildung und andere Privilegien," in *Kursbuch 143: Der Neid*, Berlin: Rowohlt, pp. 39–53.

—— (2002) *Der Mythos von den Leistungseliten. Spitzenkarrieren und soziale Herkunft in Wirtschaft, Politik, Justiz und Wissenschaft*, Frankfurt a.M.: Campus.

—— (2003) "Juristen – Abschied aus den Vorständen der Großkonzerne," in S. Machura and S. Ulbrich (eds), *Recht – Gesellschaft – Kommunikation*, Baden-Baden: Nomos, pp. 118–28.

—— (2005) "Studiengebühren und Hochschulzugang. Vorbild USA?" *Leviathan*, 33: 439–63.

Henwood, D. (1998) *Wall Street. How it works and for whom*, London and New York: Verso.

Herzog, D. (1975) *Politische Karrieren. Selektion und Professionalisierung politischer Führungsgruppen*, Opladen: Westdeutscher Verlag.

—— (1982) *Politische Führungsgruppen*, Darmstadt: Wissenschaftliche Buchgesellschaft.

—— (1990) "Der moderne Berufspolitiker. Karrierebedingungen und Funktion in westlichen Demokratien," in H.G. Wehling (ed.), *Eliten in der Bundesrepublik*, Stuttgart: Kohlhammer, pp. 28–51.

Higley, J., Hoffmann-Lange, U., Kadushin, C. and Moore, G. (1991) "Elite integration in stable democracies: a reconsideration," *European Sociological Review* 7: 35–53.

Hoffmann-Lange, U. (1990) *Eliten in der Bundesrepublik Deutschland*, Mannheim: Habilitationsschrift Universität Mannheim.

—— (1991) "West German elites: cartel of anxiety, power elite or responsive representatives?" in U. Hoffmann-Lange (ed.), *Social and Political Structures in West Germany. From Authoritarianism to Postindustrial Democracy*, Boulder: Westview Press, pp. 81–104.

—— (1992) *Eliten, Macht und Konflikt*, Opladen: Leske + Budrich.

—— (2003) "Das pluralistische Paradigma der Elitenforschung," in S. Hradil and P. Imbusch (eds), *Oberschichten – Eliten – Herrschende Klassen*, Opladen: Leske + Budrich, pp. 111–18.

——, Neumann, H. and Steinkemper, B. (1980) *Konsens und Konflikt zwischen Führungsgruppen in der Bundesrepublik Deutschland*, Frankfurt a.M.: Peter + Verlag.

Hohorst, G., Kocka, J. and Ritter, G.A. (1975) *Sozialgeschichtliches Arbeitsbuch. Materialien zur Statistik des Kaiserreichs 1870–1914*, Munich: C.H. Beck.

Höpner, M. (2003) *Wer beherrscht die Unternehmen? Shareholder Value, Managerherrschaft und Mitbestimmung in Deutschland*, Frankfurt a.M.: Campus.

Hübner, P. (1967) *Herrschende Klasse und Elite. Eine Strukturanalyse der Gesellschafts-theorien Moscas und Paretos*, Berlin: Duncker & Humblot.

Ishida, H. (1993) *Social Mobility in Contemporary Japan. Educational Credentials, Class and the Labour Market in a Cross-National Perspective*, London: Macmillan Press.

Kanter, R.M. (1995) *World Class. Thriving Locally in the Global Economy*, New York: Simon & Schuster.

Keller, S. (1963) *Beyond the Ruling Class. Strategic Elites in Modern Society*, New York: Random House.

—— (1968) *Elites*, in D.L. Sills (ed.), *International Encyclopedia of the Social Sciences*, Vol. 5, New York: The Macmillan Company and The Free Press: 26–9.

Kerbo, H.R. and McKinstry, J.A. (1995) *Who Rules Japan? The Inner Circles of Economic and Political Power*, Westport: Praeger.

Kerviel, S. (1991) "Qui devient bachelier?" *Le Monde L'Education* 179, Fevrier: 40–4.

Kesler, J.F. (1997) "L'Enarchie n'existe pas," *Pouvoirs. Revue Francaise d'etudes constitutionelles et politiques* 80: 23–41.

Kornhauser, W. (1959) *The Politics of Mass Society*, New York: Free Press of Glencoe.

Krais, B. (2001) "Die Spitzen der Gesellschaft. Theoretische Überlegungen," in B. Krais (ed.), *An der Spitze. Deutsche Eliten im sozialen Wandel*, Constance: UVK, pp. 7–62.

—— and Gebauer, G. (2002) *Habitus*, Bielefeld: transcript Verlag.

Krugman, P. (2002) "For Richer," *New York Times*, October 20.

Lasswell, H.D. (1934) *World Politics and Personal Insecurity*, Chicago: University of Chicago Press.

—— (1936) *Politics: Who Gets What, When and How*, New York: McGraw-Hill.

—— (1948) *Power and Personality*, New York: W.W. Norton.

—— and Kaplan, A. (1950) *Power and Society, A Framework for Political Inquiry*, New Haven: Yale University Press.

—— and Lerner, D. (1965) *World Revolutionary Elites. Studies in Coercive Ideological Movements*, Cambridge, Mass.: MIT Press.

Le Bon, G. (1895) *Psychologie des foules*, Paris: Alcan; Engl. *The Crowd: A Study* of *the Popular Mind*, New York: Macmillan 1896.

Leif, T. and Speth, R. (2003) *Die stille Macht. Lobbyismus in Deutschland*, Opladen: Westdeutscher Verlag.

Lerner, R., Nagai, A.K. and Rothman, S. (1996) *American Elites*, New Haven and London: Yale University Press.

Levy, A.H. (1990) *Elite Education and the Private School. Excellence and Arrogance at Phillips Exeter Academy*, Lewiston: Edwin Mellen Press.

Mann, M. (1986) *The Sources of Social Power, Vol. 1. A History of Power from the Beginning to A.D. 1760*. Cambridge: Cambridge University Press.

Mannheim, K. (1935) *Mensch und Gesellschaft im Zeitalter des Umbaus*, Leiden: Erweiterte Auflage. Bad Homburg v.d.H., Verlag Gehlen, 1967.

Marceau, J. (1977) *Class and Status in France. Economic Change and Social Immobility 1945–1975*, Oxford: Oxford University Press.

—— (1989a) *A Family Business? The Making of an International Business Elite*, Cambridge: Cambridge University Press.

—— (1989b) "International management and the class structure," in S.R. Clegg (ed.), *Organization Theory and Class Analysis: New Approaches and New Issues*, Berlin: De Gruyter, pp. 193–210.

Michels, R. (1908) "Die oligarchischen Tendenzen in der modernen Gesellschaft. Ein Beitrag zum Problem der Demokratie," *Archiv für Sozialwissenschaft und Sozialpolitik*, 27: 73–135.

—— (1911) *Zur Soziologie des Parteiwesens in der modernen Demokratie. Untersuchungen über die oligarchischen Tendenzen des Gruppenlebens*, Leipzig: Verlag Werner Klinkhardt.

Mills, C.W. (1958) "The Structure of power in American society", in *The British Journal of Sociology* 9: 29–41.

—— (1959) *The Power Elite*, New York: OUP/Galaxy Books (original printing Oxford: Oxford University Press 1956).

Mosca, G. (1896) *Elementi di Scienza Politica*, Turin: Bocca (erweiterte Auflage 1923); Engl. *The Ruling Class. Elementi de Scienza Politica*, New York: McGraw-Hill 1939.

Mougel, F.C. (1990) *Élites et système de pouvoir en Grande-Bretagne 1945–1987*, Bordeaux: Presses Universitaires de Bordeaux.

Palmade, G. (1975) *Das bürgerliche Zeitalter. Bd. 27. Fischers Weltgeschichte*, Frankfurt a.M.: Fischer Verlag; Lizenzauflage (1998) Augsburg: Weltbild Verlag.

Pareto, V. (1916) *Trattato di Sociologia generale*. Firenze: Barbera; Engl. *The Mind and Society. A Treatise on General Sociology*, New York: Dover Publications 1935.

Parsons, T. (1959) "General theory in sociology," in R.K. Merton, L. Broom and S. Cottrell Jr. (eds), *Sociology Today. Problems and Prospects*, New York: Basic Books, pp. 3–38.

Parsons, T. and Smelser, N.J (1956) *Economy and Society*, London: Routledge and Kegan Paul.

Phillips, K. (2002) *Wealth and Democracy. A Political History of the American Rich*, New York: Broadway Books.

Rebenstorf, H. (1995) *Die politische Klasse. Zur Entstehung und Reproduktion einer Funktionselite*, Frankfurt a.M.: Campus.

Riesman, D. (1953) *The Lonely Crowd*, New York: Doubleday.

Rohlen, T.P. (1983) *Japan's High Schools*, Berkeley: University of California Press.

Romano, R. and Tenenti, A. (1967) *Die Grundlegung der modernen Welt. Bd. 12. Fischers Weltgeschichte*, Frankfurt a.M.: Fischer; Lizenzauflage (1998) Augsburg: Weltbild Verlag.

Rothacher, A. (1993) *The Japanese Power Elite*, London: Macmillan Press.

Rouban, L. (1999) "The Senior Civil Service in France," in E.C. Page and V. Wright (eds), *Bureaucratic Élites in Western European States*, Oxford: Oxford University Press, pp. 65–89.

Roulin-Lefebvre, V. and Esquieu, P. (1992) *L'origine sociale des étudiants (1960–1990*, Note d'information 92.39.

Saint Martin, M. de (1993) *L'espace de la noblesse*, Paris: Éditions Métailié; Ger. *Der Adel. Soziologie eines Standes*, Constance: UVK 1993.

Schnapp, K.U. (1997a) "Soziale Zusammensetzung von Elite und Bevölkerung – Verteilung von Aufstiegschancen in die Elite im Zeitvergleich," in W. Bürklin and H. Rebenstorf (1997) *Eliten in Deutschland. Rekrutierung und Integration*, Opladen: Leske + Budrich, pp. 69–99.

—— (1997b) "Soziodemographische Merkmale der bundesdeutschen Eliten," in W. Bürklin and W. Rebenstorf (1997) *Eliten in Deutschland. Rekrutierung und Integration*, Opladen: Leske + Budrich, pp. 101–21.

Scott, J. (1991) *Who Rules Britain?* Cambridge: Polity Press.

Sklair, L. (2001) *The Transnational Capitalist Class*, Oxford: Blackwell Publishers.

Stammer, O. (1965a) "Das Elitenproblem in der Demokratie," in O. Stammer, *Politische Soziologie und Demokratieforschung. Ausgewählte Reden und Aufsätze zur Soziologie und Politik*, Berlin: Duncker & Humblot, pp. 63–90.

—— (1965b) "'Zum Elitenbegriff in der Demokratieforschung," in O. Stammer, *Politische Soziologie und Demokratieforschung. Ausgewählte Reden und Aufsätze zur Soziologie und Politik*, Berlin: Duncker & Humblot, pp. 169–82.

—— (1969) "Elite und Elitenbildung," in W. Bernsdorf (ed.), *Wörterbuch der Soziologie*, Stuttgart: Ferdinand Enke, pp. 217–20.

Suleiman, E. (1997) "Les élites de l'administration et de la politique dans la France de la V. République: Homogénéité, puissance, permanence," in E. Suleiman and H. Mendras (eds), *Le recrutement des élites en Europe*, Paris: Éditions La Découverte, pp. 19–47.

Treiman, D.J. (1977) *Occupational Prestige in Comparative Perspective*, New York: Academic Press.

Wehler, H.U. (1995) *Deutsche Gesellschaftsgeschichte. Dritter Band: Von der "Deutschen Doppelrevolution" bis zum Beginn des Ersten Weltkrieges*, Munich: C.H. Beck.

Werner, W. (2003) "Zurück in die Zeit des Great Gatsby? Änderungen in der amerikanischen Einkommensverteilung im späten 20. Jahrhundert," in W. Fluck and W. Werner (eds), *Wieviel Ungleichheit verträgt die Demokratie? Armut und Reichtum in den USA*, Frankfurt a.M.: Campus, pp. 23–46.

Wildenmann, R., Kaase, M., Hoffmann-Lange, U., Kutteroff, A. and Wolf, G. (1982) *Führungsschicht in der Bundesrepublik Deutschland*, Mannheim: Universität Mannheim.

Zapf, W. (1965a) *Wandlungen der deutschen Elite*, Munich: R. Piper & Co.

—— (1965b) "Führungsgruppen in West- und Ostdeutschland," in W. Zapf (ed.), *Beiträge zur Analyse der deutschen Oberschicht*, Munich: R. Piper & Co., pp. 9–29.

—— (1965c) "Die deutschen Manager. Sozialprofil und Karriereweg," in W. Zapf (ed.), *Beiträge zur Analyse der deutschen Oberschicht*, Munich: R. Piper & Co., pp. 136–49.

—— (ed.) (1971) *Theorien des sozialen Wandels*, Cologne: Kiepenheuer & Witsch.

Index